Magnificent Leadership

Magnificent Leadership

Transform Uncertainty, Transcend Circumstance, Claim the Future

Sarah Levitt

BUSINESS EXPERT PRESS

Magnificent Leadership: Transform Uncertainty, Transcend Circumstance, Claim the Future

Copyright © Business Expert Press, LLC, 2018.

First published in 2018 by
Business Expert Press, LLC
222 East 46th Street, New York, NY 10017
www.businessexpertpress.com

ISBN-13: 978-1-63157-716-1 (paperback)
ISBN-13: 978-1-63157-717-8 (e-book)

Business Expert Press Human Resource Management and Organizational Behavior Collection

Collection ISSN: 1946-5637 (print)
Collection ISSN: 1946-5645 (electronic)

Cover and interior design by Exeter Premedia Services Private Ltd., Chennai, India

First edition: 2018

10 9 8 7 6 5 4 3 2 1

Printed in the United States of America.

To the magnificence that dwells within us all

Abstract

A must read for CEOs and senior business executives who wish to transform and transcend circumstance. Magnificent Leadership® is the culmination of the author's interviews with leadership exemplars across all different domains for The Making Magnificence Project®. Inviting you into the unique leadership journeys that she captured, the author distills the essential elements of leadership success gleaned during her interviews. Both senior leaders and the general population can use this book as a guide and resource for leading through uncertainty and living in aspiration. Although well suited for business executives leading in high stakes, chaotic environments, this book is for anyone who hopes to create something greater from circumstance and claim the future.

Keywords

aspiration, business coaching, business, CEO coaching, C-suite, executive coaching, executive development, executive performance, high performing teams, innovation, leadership development, leadership, leading through change, learning, Magnificent Leadership®, resilience, self-development, self-mastery, strategic focus, The Making Magnificence Project®, transformation, transition, uncertainty

Contents

Praise for *Magnificent Leadership*

Sarah Levitt, with sensitive and keen insight, illuminates the crucial elements of leadership and personal mastery in this touching compilation of individual leadership journeys to magnificence. A great read for all leaders and leaders-to-be.

—Marshall Goldsmith
New York Times #1 bestselling author of *Triggers*
and *What Got You Here Won't Get You There*

Sarah Levitt is a terrific coach and now a terrific author. Magnificent Leadership isn't just a wonderful collection of personal stories on achievement, it's a practical guidebook for strong leadership and success.

—Matthew Lepore
Senior Vice President and General Counsel,
Chief Compliance Officer, BASF Corporation

Sarah Levitt has beautifully threaded universal leadership themes uncovered across a diverse group of successful men and women. Each narrative provides something that I can relate to as a CEO as well as offers inspiration towards qualities that I aspire towards. Quick, easy read that helped to reorganize my personal priorities.

—Doug Satzman
CEO, Joe Coffee Company

Sarah has used her coaching wisdom and curiosity to present magnificent human beings in a light that inspires the reader. Her storytelling finesse and focus on what is at the heart of greatness connects the reader to every chapter. The methodical approach to Sarah's writing and real life examples of magnificence make her book a wonderful manual of what every person can be if we reach inside ourselves and harness our own light.

—Lori Patton
Chief Learning Officer, Womble Bond Dickinson (US) LLP

Acknowledgments

My heartfelt gratitude first and foremost goes to those people who have participated in, and continue to join, The Making Magnificence Project®. I am deeply, deeply grateful to them for sharing their stories. Without their generosity and courage, the Project would only have been an idea and this book would never have existed.

The enormous blessing of my grandmother's love continues to ripple out over my life. She was a model of magnificence, and I once told her that I would write about her life. Perhaps, in some way, this is that book. Thank you, Gertie.

There have been so very many friends and colleagues who have been on my path these last years, who influenced my journey, and who, more recently, provided moral support as I wrote and from whom I've benefitted by knowing. People who assured me that I could do it, who encouraged, inquired, and cheered me on. There are far too many to name here, but I am so grateful to them all.

My thanks also goes to Gretchen Pisano, an early mentor, who saw me launch The Making Magnificence Project® and suggested the thoughtful question "The best advice you never got?" It has been, and remains, the last question I ask of everyone I interview.

I have been fortunate to have had many great teachers; among them, Martha Beck, Rob Ferguson, Terry Real, and Alan Weiss. They have made me better, professionally and personally.

I will always be grateful to Mr. George Miller, Jr., whose quiet support and unfailing belief in me has been of great comfort.

I owe a gigantic debt of gratitude to Scott Isenberg of Business Expert Press whose patience and understanding were exceedingly generous. It is not an exaggeration to say that this book made it into the world because of him.

To my extraordinary clients, leaders all: I am so very glad that we get the opportunity to work together. It is an honor and privilege to be a part of your path. I learn from you, too.

And to Laureen Golden, best friend, vision holder, and without whom I would likely not be in the same place. Your steadfast love, support, and presence are once-in-a-lifetime gifts, and I am so profoundly grateful that serendipity smiled on us 25 years ago when our dogs met and said hello. Your life has made all the difference in mine.

Finally, to Moose, Pascha, Bear, and Sagie. What gifts you've given me. Thank you.

Introduction

Before it was this book, The Making Magnificence Project® was a yearning to understand. In the early spring of 2009, life as I knew it essentially went into a blender. After my long marriage dissolved, I exited the business we'd built, a greenhouse operation begun from scratch and grown to success over 15 years, and the home we'd made, located at the greenhouse. In the ensuing 13 months, I would have to put down both of my beloved older dogs in short succession of one another. Save for two dear friends, I was as close to anchorless as I'd ever been. And there was a blank canvas in front of me.

I read a lot of memoir during that time, and although the details of those other lives didn't always exactly mirror those of my own, their stories provided a potent combination of sustenance and inspiration. It was some time later, as my new career and life began to take shape working with senior executives in the business world, that I remembered the power of story and, in particular, its companionship. Inside that companionship, a path forward often resides. Another's story can birth our own.

So I created The Making Magnificence Project® and began interviewing people who had navigated significant upheaval. I wanted to put together a collection of narratives that explored the themes of transition and resilience, transcendence and transformation. But then something happened: The deeper I went into peoples' stories, the broader my perspective became. I realized that while there were seismic events that thrust some people into chaos and impose new directions, other individuals forge paths under less tumultuous, but no less significant circumstances. And with no less determination. Making magnificence, it turns out, is a lifelong journey. Transformation is an ongoing process. And transition and uncertainty are attendant to any path.

Thus, in these pages, you'll find many types of narratives. The stories, all from my interviews for The Making Magnificence Project®, feature leaders in their fields across a wide range of domains and disciplines, including an elderly widow who was leading an extraordinary life at age

91 when I interviewed her. For those who sat at the helm of organizations, as do my clients, I wanted to hear how they led into the future when the present is characterized in most industries as turbulent, chaotic, and uncertain. How did they make decisions and set direction for their organizations, particularly in the face of the unknown? What were their influences? How did they lead themselves? What did they believe leadership was? Where did it intersect with driving business outcomes? How did they build resilience in the face of grinding performance pressure?

No matter someone's story, I used three tools that a qualitative researcher might: curiosity, questions, and listening. I asked how individuals got from one place to another, what brought them to a critical juncture. Once there, what did they do to orient themselves and chart a course? What served them best along the way? How did they face obstacles and impediments and not become derailed? Or did they? And what then? How did they take steps when the stakes were high and the outcome was long yet to be determined? I sought to understand someone's internal process as much as their external path.

While it's true that most of the interviewees from The Making Magnificence Project® have achieved significant success, accomplishment by itself isn't very instructional, and while I was happy to laud the achievements of the people I interviewed, my intention was to demystify the glittery exterior of success and show as full a picture as possible. As it came into focus, that picture included continued iteration and stumbling, triumph and setback, and disappointment and doubt, no matter how far someone had ascended.

After conducting more than 25 interviews, I began exploring how these stories might relate to one another. What did a critically acclaimed, award-winning writer, the ninth dean of the United States Air Force (USAF) Academy, and the CEO of a multibillion dollar company have in common? They'd all successfully transcended significant challenge and difficult circumstances to create something greater. Yes. But was there more? As I stepped back, themes began to emerge from this seemingly disparate collection. In the end, there were eight threads that ran through the stories. Those threads weave a vibrant picture of living in aspiration, which I've come to understand as the essence of Magnificent Leadership®.

Each chapter features narratives that best exemplify and highlight one of the eight key factors of Magnificent Leadership®, even though many, if not most, of the factors are often found in an individual's story. To put these factors to work for you, there is a chapter at the end of the book with opportunities for practical application to yourself, first, and then, if you're in a leadership position, to your team and organization.

If leadership's measure is in part defined by courage, you'll find that it runs deep among the narratives in these pages, not only in the stories themselves, but in the generosity of the people who shared them. My gratitude is truly inestimable. And The Making Magnificence Project® continues on with more interviews. Information can be found on my website: www.sarah-levitt.com.

No matter your path's direction or arc, my wish is that these stories keep you good company. We are all leading through change. We are all finding our way through uncertainty. And we all hope to transcend and transform circumstance into something greater, into magnificence.

CHAPTER 1

Passion Married to a High Tolerance for Uncertainty

Featured Narrative: Ben Fountain, Writer

Even though it can be tough out there on your own, there's also this kind of fierce pride that comes along with it. You haven't taken the safe route, you haven't taken the easy route. You're trying to do something that's really unusual and hard, and may be worthwhile someday. But at least you didn't settle for the safe, easy thing.

There is no arguing that Ben Fountain's work has captured the kind of critical acclaim reserved for writers of great talent and achievement. Among the honors: a PEN/Hemingway Award, two Pushcart Prizes, a National Book Critics Circle Award, and an O. Henry Prize. His novel *Billy Lynn's Long Halftime Walk* was a National Book Award finalist and has been made into a movie directed by Ang Lee. He's been called a genius in Malcolm Gladwell's *New Yorker* article.[1] The accolades are many.

But his success was not overnight. It wasn't even over a decade. A teenager when he first "conceived the notion of maybe trying to write," Ben looked toward his future and instead chose law school. There were many lawyers in his family; it was a known path. And the prospect of succeeding at writing seemed so small. There was the hard work of it, yes, but there was the risk of investing himself in a pursuit that required more than diligence and effort. Writing demanded "some spark of talent," Ben explains. And, the only way to know if you had it was to dive in, and, as

---

[1] Gladwell, M. 2008. "Late Bloomers." *The New Yorker*, October 20.

he shares during our interview, "Nobody wants to waste their life." So, law school, it was. And, initially, after he graduated and was practicing, he looked back on the notion to write as an "adolescent aspiration," as something he would never do.

But then, five years into his legal career, the desire to write reached up from within. Except that Ben was no longer an adolescent. He was a man with a career and a marriage and a kid. But. "It wasn't letting go of me," Ben recalls, "and I finally realized I was never going to have any peace in myself if I didn't make a serious attempt to do this kind of work." So he talked with his trusted partner and emotional support, his wife. They made a plan: Her attorney's salary would be their income and they'd get a nanny to come in to take care of their son. And Ben would write. Every day.

"It was really completely insane to do this," Ben shares with me. "In one sense, I mean, totally irresponsible and a huge risk." He was abandoning his income in favor of an altogether unknown, uncharted path. When he left the law firm and they told him he'd be back in six months, he couldn't deny that as a real possibility. But despite thinking that he could never, would never, resign the law after his first child was born, Ben says, "The exact opposite happened." He remembers looking at his son and thinking, "Maybe the best thing I can do is to be true to myself, or whole in myself." It turned out that having a child was "the final push" to write, rather than the obstacle. It had convinced him.

But he was starting from scratch. At 30 years old, Ben was a beginner. Something he describes as "daunting, and somewhat humiliating and embarrassing." Aside from a bit of writing during college and the summer before law school, he was "in first grade all over again." He was learning to write. But at the outset, he first had to become a student of his own mind and discern how he would work. The years as an attorney taught him that he had the capacity for 16-hour days, but how would he apply that to writing? Would he immerse himself for several days with alternating time off? Or would he sit at the kitchen table each day, for hours? It would be a year and a half before he understood that he had to be at the kitchen table. He had structure and place and was building his stamina. He just needed the writing.

"Those first three or four years, pretty much everything I wrote, I was disgusted by," Ben recalls. But he knew that if he was going to get to the other side, he had to continue. "I guess I just sensed instinctively the only way I would ever get to the point where I might write something decent, was by writing out all this bad stuff," he says. It would be a decade before he could capture the essential emotional experience of whatever it was that he was trying to write, no longer, as he says, "skimming along the surface." Save for some minor successes during that period, short stories intermittently and infrequently published in "small, obscure magazines," Ben wrote with little acknowledgment or affirmation. After showing up and writing every day, for hours, with additional time stolen on weekends, he shares, "I turned forty and I had very little to show for the ten years of writing."

I wonder: How did he keep showing up at that kitchen table? How did he continue on?

Certainly, at first glance, there is the extraordinary passion that drove and sustained Ben's commitment to writing. To describe it as unwavering devotion would seem inadequate. His journey, in many ways, is a study in perseverance, determination, and fortitude, which could only be fueled by infinite desire. And if we looked no further or more deeply to understand his success, the portrait of a man setting out on a quest to fulfill this longing would be accurate. But it would not be complete. Because after we adjust to the clear, bright light of the fire to write, there is something else in Ben's story that asks for our attention, something far less visible but equally powerful, something that not only kept him afloat as a writer, but alive.

For a long time, Ben felt suspended, having embarked but not arrived, assiduously working, "every once in a while writing a decent sentence or a decent paragraph," and not knowing if his work would ever find a home in the world, if it would ever be met with critical reception. And it is not difficult to imagine that had he succumbed to the gnawing uncertainty that permeates this realm, a place defined by the absence of any hint or forecast of the future, we might never have read his work. But he didn't merely tolerate the "psychological, societal and maybe even spiritual limbo" he found himself in. He created some of his best work within it.

"I think fantasy and delusion, you know, let's not underestimate the power of that," Ben is saying with dry humor. I've asked what he did during this period of limbo to make it easier or more difficult. I want to know how he sustained himself, how he kept writing, through the uncertainty and the unknown. Looking back, he thought that small successes would become larger, would become turning points. Getting a couple of short stories published in short succession was promising. Getting a first agent, even more so. "I'm like a camel crossing the desert, I can go a long way without a drink of water," Ben says. Every triumph, however small, provided some confirmation that this was possible, that he had the talent. And, too, he began to understand "that a good deal of life is failure." Putting his work out into the world and having it rejected was what he had chosen, and over time, he learned that he could withstand the rejections, that he was able to "take the hits and keep on going."

There are those writers who meet success early, whether by talent or luck, but most, he says, endure a long haul. And for them and for him, "Eventually, it has to become about the work," he explains. It is here, in the many years of living and working in the place of between, that something significant shifted for Ben in the way that he looked at himself and his work. And it was a change in perspective that was necessary, he tells me. Approaching his 40th birthday, he made a decision:

> About eight or nine years in, I got kind of Zen about it. I decided I wasn't going to do anything else. I wasn't going to go back to practicing law, I wasn't going to go to business school and get my MBA. This is what I was going to do. I was all in. . . . And if I never had any success to speak of, well, I made my peace with that.

He was going to show up at the kitchen table. And just write.

Over and over again, Ben's mettle would be tested. What he didn't know during those years of limbo was that there would be no turning point, no momentum. Not then. In fact, the disappointments were bruising. His first agent dropped him after two years because he wasn't developing fast enough. He completed a novel, five years in the making, and his second agent was unable to sell it. Ben told him, "Pull it in. Let's just put it in the drawer." As one decade rolled into two, 17 years after Ben left the law to write, he received his first book contract for a collection of short stories, *Brief Encounters With Che Guevara*, and a novel. *Brief Encounters* received critical acclaim, and he was featured in Gladwell's article. But six weeks after appearing in *The New Yorker*, his second novel, also with years invested and multiple rounds of revisions, was rejected. His editor said it wasn't good enough, that he could do better. Ben says, "If I was tempted to think I was over the hump, that set me straight really quickly." It would be 2012 before he would finally publish *Billy Lynn's Long Halftime Walk*. That novel received the National Book Critics Circle Award for Fiction and the Flaherty-Dunnan First Novel Prize, and was a National Book Award finalist.

Reflecting on his path, Ben does not shy away from the fact that it was taxing. "It takes a psychological toll and an emotional toll. And I don't think that that part of the experience is to be underestimated," he says. Writing asked a lot of him. There were times when he was difficult to live with, times when he was frustrated. He recalls going "through these periods of existential crisis and angst," and the support of his wife was essential. She "never, ever expressed doubt," he says. Nor did she ever complain that he was bringing in so little income.

Looking back, he tells me that he doesn't think his success should have happened any sooner. His writing simply wasn't there yet, didn't merit the attention. When his work got better, better things started happening. He has no complaints as to how things unfolded. If there is anything that he would do differently, it would be "to come to an appreciation, sooner than I did, of the virtue and pleasure in focusing on the work itself." That required time. As I take in the whole of Ben's journey, it strikes me that perhaps its essence is best captured in what happened after each of his first two novels was rejected. He tells me that on both occasions, he got up the next morning and thought, "Well, I still get to write."

CHAPTER 2

The Lens We Look Through: Framing and Reframing

Featured Narrative: Dan Michelson, CEO, Strata Decision Technology

I actually never had an objective to be a CEO, I never thought I would be a CEO, and never interviewed for a CEO position until the one I'm in right now. I guess I'm sort of an accidental CEO.

A self-described recluse during high school and a mediocre athlete at best, Dan Michelson was often an observer, someone on the outside looking in. His parents divorced when he was two years old, when his mother was an unemployed schoolteacher with only a few hundred dollars in her bank account. Now about to turn 50, Dan hasn't seen his father in 40 years. Upon graduating from college, Dan tells me,

> My only real goal in life was to have a place of my own at some point. I really didn't have much confidence or much of a plan. I wouldn't say I didn't have any ambition, but I just didn't think too highly of myself and where I would end up.

But end up, he did. Once among those last picked for sports teams in high school, the CEO of Strata Decision Technology has run 15 marathons, among them, the elite Boston Marathon, for which he qualified six times, and a Chicago marathon where he placed among the top 150 runners. Married and a father of two teenagers, he and his wife founded a nonprofit, Project Music, which raises money to send children living in a group home in Chicago to overnight camp. He has excelled in business and leadership. Dan was a member of the core executive team that took Allscripts, a small health care information technology company, from 26 million dollars in revenue to over 1.4 billion. Now the CEO of Strata, under Dan's leadership the company has quadrupled in size. After being brought in as its CEO, he led the company to sale a few years later for $140 million.

So what happened in those intervening years? Did Dan Michelson rebuild himself, creating a superman capable of running long distances and leading companies? Or did he become himself, finding a natural home for his talents? How, exactly, did he get from there to here, I want to know. How did a kid without much confidence, who once had a difficult time making conversation at the dinner table, become a CEO who regularly conveys meaning and context to those whom he leads?

"I think my twenties were really a turning point for me," Dan shares during our interview. His natural curiosity drew him to new experiences, and looking back, he doesn't know if it was a skill he'd always had or that he just liked to work really hard, but running, and running long distances, suited him. One day's three-mile run turned into six. Before long, he'd signed up to run a half-marathon and then a full. He was happy to finish that first 26.2-mile race. By his third attempt, he was among those top 150 marathon finishers in Chicago. And although he'd stumbled into it somewhat, marathon running would become one of the significant "marbles in the jar" of experiences that built his confidence. And, too, there was the grad school professor whose teachings on communication gave him more skill and greater ease. Dan recalls,

> There were a number of epiphanies during the two classes that I took with him that both opened me up and gave me some more confidence to tell my story even though I didn't feel like I had much of a story to tell.

Professional life after college took him from an initial entry-level position in sales to ascending rungs at different organizations, each with increasing responsibility, culminating in his role as Chief Marketing and

Strategy Officer at Allscripts. He would be there for 12 years. "We were literally trying to create a company and an industry at the same time. It's an incredibly difficult thing to do," Dan explains. The challenges built his confidence, the mistakes and successes informed his learnings. When he got the call to join Strata as its CEO, he was intrigued. Years earlier, he'd chosen health care as the sphere in which he wanted to make his career, make an impact. "It's a huge set of problems and there's a human element to it," Dan says. One of the requirements of the job was taking a 50 percent pay cut. But, he'd taken a cut in salary when he joined Allscripts, and when I ask him about the risk, particularly at this time in his life, he says,

> I just want to work on things that are interesting to me and that are big problems that I think need to be solved, where I think I can make a difference and where I'm working with people who I really like and respect. And that set of principles was in place both times where I made a decision.

Perhaps, more than anything, he finally convinced himself that he was ready to learn something new and take on some risk.

But that perspective and his confidence weren't solely the product of the experiences he'd collected or the communication skills he'd acquired. Shoved into his wallet were pieces of paper filled with "mantras," as Dan called them, quotes written in his small handwriting that he found personally meaningful and that he'd been writing down since his 20s. One of his favorites "Barn's burnt down, now I can see the moon"[1] spoke to seeing bad things as good things. Whether he knew it at the time, he had carefully been grinding the lens through which he looked. Its shape was defined by "getting excited about where you're at versus down about where you've been, or distracted by where you're going, but to live in the now and be excited about it," Dan tells me. And that lens, one that seems to blend his contrarianism, pragmatism, and hope for what is possible, even in the midst of struggle, allows him to frame and reframe, to turn

---

[1] Mizuta Masahide, Haiku, 17th century.

things upside down and take another look, to very deliberately choose how he will think about and approach challenge. It is the lens he looks through as CEO as he guides his team at Strata. Dan says,

> We have situations here where things can get really tough, as every company does. I always counsel people that when they encounter something really challenging, they are lucky and it is awesome. Now, when they get to the other side of this, which they will, they're going to have that experience of having worked through something that was really hard. The next time they walk down that street, they're going to recognize what it looks like, and know where to step and where not to. If things had gone smoothly, they would never have had that experience, and that would have been a huge miss.

It is in this role as CEO that the whole of his experiences came together to inform his leadership. His natural curiosity and his proclivity for finding and liking to work on "things that are in the gray," as he describes it, were tremendous assets. He saw and created vital new markets for Strata where competitors weren't looking. And, yes, some of the experiences of his childhood were painful. But the emotional weight that he carried as a kid, the experience of being an outsider and an observer, gave him a sense of people that was crucial to leadership. "It's made me much more empathetic as a leader," he says. Even the insecurity was helpful. It pushed him to strive, to want to become better. Those challenges had been exceptional preparation for the requirements of being a CEO. And it's clear during our conversation that Dan has spent time considering what it means to sit in that seat and to be a leader.

"In addition to going through their own reviews and evaluations, everyone on our team does a performance review of me," Dan says. His review is blinded, it's qualitative and quantitative, and he shares the results with others. He quite purposefully wants to set the tone that "everyone, from top to bottom, is always working on things that they could be better at." The idea is to change the mindset from a traditional review, in this case, Dan says, by "putting the onus on the employee to want, and need to, have that coaching and feedback, while providing me as the example."

If managers don't give team members at least two things to work on, they're not doing their job.

Dan emphasizes that feedback must be connected to context, to the meaning of someone's work. It is not an extra, a layer of icing, at Strata; it is essential. He explains:

> Merely presenting a scoreboard to somebody at a point in time but them not being able to tie that back to what they're doing on a daily basis, or what they're doing within the throes of the game, is useless. That lack of context is crippling to both the individual and the organization.

And meaning is not always about the scoreboard. He is known to go out of his way to explain to the team how their contributions are important. "Just those simple things, the little things, end up mattering a ton. And context is king. You have to be maniacal about it."

Framing is as important for success as it is for challenge, Dan tells me. "What we're trying to do at Strata is bend the cost curve in health care, and that's a pretty ambitious thing to work on," he says. Business is a roller coaster, and while achievement is celebrated, it's never taken for granted. Things can change quickly and being "able to prepare people for the other side of that" is crucial, he says. Those who thrive in a continually changing, and challenging, business climate, who enjoy the "constant process of tweaking and iterating and improving," will likely enjoy the journey.

Although Dan has chosen the lens he looks through, it has not shielded him against some of life's more painful events. He is careful to point out that adversity still visits him, that there have been significant personal trials. "My family dealt with some pretty tough issues over the last couple of years," he tells me. His wife had breast cancer, and the man who became his father after his mother remarried, who was the best man at Dan's own wedding, battled melanoma. "Those are really, really tough, but they are also reminders as to what a privilege it is to work in health care and try to make a difference," he says.

Toward the end of our interview, as he considers the whole of his journey and the boy who was once a recluse, Dan thinks back to the teacher in high school who saw his potential that Dan could not and the tremendous difference that it made. Finding people who believe in us is crucial, he says. He understands now that the best bet is the one that you make on yourself, although he's not sure he would have understood it at the time. If there is anything that would have been more helpful, it might have been to have had more experiences early on, because one simply doesn't know what might transpire from them. He says,

> Just go through as many doors as you can, and grab as many experiences as you can, doing as many different things as you can. It doesn't have to be from a work perspective. Pursue your passions and integrate them into your life.

Although he never expected to become a CEO, I wonder if Dan found his place, one where his talents and experiences, all of them, combine with his efforts to the greatest impact and effect. And I wonder if the person who fought to interpret the events of his life in such a way that he could move forward isn't ideally suited for a role that is infinitely challenging and where others look to him for direction and guidance. Dan says,

> People search for meaning, in their work, and in their daily lives just in general. Being able to provide that context is incredibly, incredibly important. As a leader, I don't know if there's a more important part of the job.

As for his own direction, inside Dan's wallet are those pieces of paper from his 20s. And he continues to add more.

CHAPTER 3

Accepting What Is to Create What Can Be

Featured Narrative: Selma Ungar, 91-Year-Old Widow

I do change with the times; I don't stay stuck with old habits.

"I get down like everybody else does. Believe me," Selma Ungar is assuring me. We've been talking about her exuberance for life at a stage when many might choose to relinquish aspiration. I want to understand how she thrives in the midst of tumult and loss, rather than retreating and permitting those circumstances to define the outer parameters of her life. Because, the fact is, the configuration of Selma's life has changed dramatically from what it once was. In some ways, that life was not atypical or unusual, despite its richness. She had a long marriage, raised a family, helped her husband in his business when needed, and eagerly volunteered for causes she cared about. There were challenges, of course, twists and turns, the marital bumps when she considered leaving, the financial pressures of owning a business when she and her husband "were both ready to throw everything away." But when I interviewed her, most of those defining anchors in her life were gone. She was widowed and her children were long grown. Volunteering was more difficult and less of a fixture. In their place, Selma had created something else, something altogether different. And while this might be a feat for anyone, the reconstruction of a life, I'm particularly interested in how she's doing it at this time and place. Because, at 91, Selma is going to the gym every day, driving a red convertible, and doing online dating.

"Things change and I change with them," Selma's telling me. I'm trying to understand how she remains so incredibly nimble, asking how she embraces life so fully. I could mistake her answer as wholly incomplete rather than the profound statement that it is, but she actually lives these words. Technology? "I couldn't live without a computer, I can tell you that," she says. Whether corresponding with suitors, watching streaming, playing bridge, or checking in on friends, many scattered throughout the United States and some ailing, to daily share the details of life, her computer is both disruptor of loneliness and conduit to connection. "We know every little thing that's happening," she says of those friendships maintained over the ether. She doesn't believe there's anything intentional that she's doing to cultivate this zest for living and says that she's "always just enjoyed anything that's happening in life." I could well imagine that her vitality and adaptability might simply be a part of who she is. And has always been.

But, her elasticity is no accident, her finesse a choice. As Selma shares her story, and I try to deconstruct the grace with which she maneuvers through change, I discover a wealth of skill and deliberate resilience. Whether it's that she never really paid much attention to aging until her 90th birthday—that one, she said, "sounded awfully old, and I don't feel that way"—or that she combines the optimism of making new friends with the poignant understanding that they may not be long relationships—"Some of the support system's leaving because everybody's dying"—Selma has a chosen a way of looking at things that enables her to focus on what's helpful, let go of what's not, and take action where it most matters.

But that wasn't always the case. Aging, she tells me, has imparted a gift. Despite what it takes away, growing older has given Selma a tranquility that eluded her in years past. Stories from her younger days provide a window. There was the teapot purchased on her first wedding anniversary that read, "Don't worry, it may never happen," a gift from her husband. The challenges she doesn't think she "could have weathered" without his reassuring presence. The annoyances with people whom she would decide to "have nothing to do with." But that has changed. She has changed. Time and experience have granted her a different perspective: "I found one thing as you get older, I think you accept more."

As we explore this notion of acceptance, I wonder if it is, paradoxically, the fuel for Selma's adaptability. I wonder if it's her secret weapon.

Because she's not just talking about being better at letting go of the irritations of people and their quirks, although those, too, rarely bother her any more. She's referring to accepting change itself, and the circumstances it dictates, almost always without her consent. She has found a way to relax into what is. In a different person, acceptance might be in danger of becoming resignation. But in Selma, it is propulsion toward what is still yet. With her gaze steadily fixed on what's possible rather than lamenting what has been, she says, "I'm always getting involved in something." There are her creative endeavors like painting, which fill the walls of her house; social outings where she's known for never returning "home from anywhere without having a friend or knowing their life history"; and her "real love" of cooking, which sends her into the kitchen whenever she's upset. All of this is in addition to her regimen at the gym, dating, and keeping up with friends and family.

If there is any sadness for what once was, it is volunteering with regularity and consistency. She reminisces about the organizations she presided over as president, fondly remembering a fundraising campaign that provided wheelchairs to those in need. Confessing that she was always more an ideas than details person, she never shied away from "being the one to go ask people for money." During the somewhat difficult transition of increasingly working more in her husband's business, when the kids were young, she found herself unable to participate in many of the activities she'd always enjoyed and "kind of broke away from everybody." It was volunteering that gave her something that she loved again, as she threw herself into fundraising in the schools and "became friendly with people all over the country."

But gone is the time when she can dive into a cause, full-on. She's had to scale back, adjust.

> That is such a lonely spot. I mean, I'd give anything to be, you know, helping. But at this stage you just can't count on what days you can go and stay so many hours. . . . But that I miss. Oh, I miss being able to do for other people.

Even here, Selma has rearranged what was into what can be. As we talk, she's making flower pens and recently took "a whole bunch to the doctor's office . . . just giving them out to everybody." Last year was the fundraiser for breast cancer when she crafted necklaces fashioned from men's ties. And, for several years, knowing that she didn't want to be president of the friendship club in her community, she was instead simply calling "everybody that was new and trying to make them feel welcome." Although the circumstances of her health are less reliable than they once were, she says that if there's "a problem somewhere, I'm the first one even now, you know, that will go . . . and do something."

It would be an omission not to acknowledge volunteering for the significant ingredient it is in Selma's enduring enthusiasm. Despite most of life's external markers having shape-shifted, leaving her with less rather than more, volunteering remains. Yes, it has changed, been curtailed, but her desire to help others and contribute seems to simultaneously moor and invigorate her. "I get more out of it than I'm actually giving," Selma reports. "I mean, I know I'm giving a lot, but there's such satisfaction." She may adore cooking, but contributing to the lives of others might be the thing that feeds her.

How does she keep her sights trained on what can still be, I want to know? How does she maintain such a hopeful focus? She tells me,

> Years ago, I wondered why my mother never got excited if I told her an old friend died, or something. Usually you hear "Oh my God, so-and-so died," and you're all upset. She just kind of took it and rolled with the punches. And, I think maybe I'm doing that. I feel so sad about it, but then I think of all the ones that are living . . . and you've got to be grateful for it.

As she shares this, I think about all the times I've read about the benefits of gratitude and how it seems to be a way of thinking for Selma and a part of her adaptation formula. I consider that although adaptable might be an accurate descriptor of Selma, it seems meager and incomplete for what she's accomplished at this stage in life, a time when so much more is taken than replenished. She claims not to be able to give anyone a recipe for what she creates in her kitchen, cooking as she does "just by feel, not by rules," but I wonder if she does, in fact, possess one master recipe from which she creates all else. And I wonder if it looks something like this: Acceptance + Focus on Possibility + Action = Living Courage.

There is one aspect of life that has remained untouched by time, Selma explains. We've been talking about dating at 91, particularly online dating, and it's a bit like two girlfriends swapping stories, despite the almost half century that separates us. "Nothing changes," she reports. Biting the inside of my cheek, I stifle a giggle as I hear the spunk in her voice. Was it intimidating, I want to know? Particularly after being married for so long? I'm in awe of her ease with all this. She waited three years before plunging in. Cautious at first, she tried researching prospective beaus online, but could find little more than if they'd done jail time, so she gave that up. She sensed something was "suspicious" with her very first online admirer despite his e-mails that had "all the sweet things we all want to hear." A mutual friend confirmed her instinct: The man had a wife in the next room as he typed. Other than that first bad apple, the men she's met have been nothing but "lovely, lovely people." And while health concerns sometimes intrude, cutting short a budding romance, she still hears from them all. Her biggest discovery about dating at this time in life? "It's not much different than when we were teenagers," she relays. Dexterous though she may be with online dating and romance at 91, there is one area of life, perhaps the sole jurisdiction, where Selma insists that she won't budge: "I've never paid for a cup of coffee with a man, and I'm not about to. But I'm old-fashioned."

CHAPTER 4

Magnificence Is Not a Solo Journey: Finding Someone to Hold the Vision

Featured Narrative: Tim Toterhi, Founder, Plotline Leadership

Sometimes your mentors know exactly what you need.

When the brass knuckles met his face, it was with enough force to knock him to the ground. Twenty years old, Tim Toterhi had been hit many times before. It had been nearly a decade since he'd first wandered into the neighborhood karate class where Sensei Sara had taken him in and put him in the dojo with adults. But this was different. This was the street, and the attack had been planned. Tapped on the shoulder from behind, he'd been mistaken for someone else that night. It was "devastating," he recalls during our interview. But as brutal as the physical assault, and as ravaging as the financial fallout without health insurance, that event, more than the lousy neighborhoods that he'd grown up in, more than the dyslexia that had made test taking impossible in school, put his future in jeopardy. Because, for the first time since he'd been practicing martial arts and slowly creating a trajectory to a new life, Tim was in doubt. It was, in his words, "a huge setback that tested kind of everything that I had been taught up to that point about what was possible."

Tim recalls with certainty that he was 12 years old when he first walked into the martial arts school. "Amazed," as he was, "at what was going on in that dojo," he couldn't help but stick around. Sensei Sara had invited him into her adult classes that met several times each week. And discerning the economics of his situation, she reduced his fee. But even still, Tim remembers, "There were certain times when three bucks wasn't possible." So, instead, Sensei gave him a job sweeping up and helping out at the school in exchange for classes. It would be years before he realized there was a janitorial staff to take care of those duties. The dojo would become more than a place to go after school, more than merely something to keep him out of trouble. It became a portal to a different life.

"The challenge that I faced at that time was I could only see one path," Tim tells me, reflecting back to the period before he met Sensei Sara. That path meant that a friend might leave an afternoon's game of playing cards with a vague reference to having to "go do this thing." Tim knew that in the Bronx and the neighborhoods just outside of New York City that he called home, those words could have different meanings, likely none of them good. And despite the worry over groceries and the challenges of life at home, Tim tells me that the greatest impediment to a different future other than what the neighborhood offered was to get "out of your own frame of reference." That was the most difficult part of composing a different life. It was also the most essential. Sure, the obvious right choice was to "go to school, and get an education, and do that sort of thing and take a different road," Tim explains. But there was a nearly insurmountable challenge. "You have to see that that's actually possible," he tells me.

At the dojo, for the first time in his life, Tim was witnessing firsthand "what success could look like." He watched as people in class would "go from knowing nothing about an endeavor to actually making progress and moving through the ranks." Success was there, in front of him. He could see it. And surrounded, as he was, by adults, the dojo was a crystal ball of sorts where he could "flash forward" to what his own decisions in the present might mean for his future. He watched and listened as former students returned to class to put their lives back together after wrong turns, while others came back and spoke about reaping the "dividends" of staying the course. Sensei's first gift, he tells me, was showing him a different path for his life. Her second, he emphasizes, was teaching him how to have "the discipline and rigor to choose it every day."

The wooden floor of the dojo was also a teacher. On it, he practiced. Over and over again, he faced adults who were bigger, stronger, and more experienced, honing his martial arts skills, but perhaps more crucially, becoming conditioned to facing seemingly overwhelming challenge. That lesson, of how to "embrace your circumstances and the reality of what they are" he contrasts to the "fluff" he'd heard espoused from some who, even if well meaning, would talk about "motivation" but leave him at a loss for how, exactly, to change his life. Tim explains: "That whole concept of limitations and not having any, I thought was actually kind of harmful." The mat acknowledged limitations and obstacles, even put them on display. And then it asked that he answer the question: "What do I have to do to go around the rock?" Over time, he explains, that became a new way of thinking. But its sum total was much more than a good habit. It was a new frame of reference.

"I always used to joke, I had more points on my license than I had on the SAT," Tim tells me with wry humor that often leaves me laughing during our interview. Despite adhering to Sensei's expectation that he "go to school, go to class, go to do the right thing," dyslexia had presented its own set of challenges. "Bs and Ds don't make for good test-taking," he shares. But, there were teachers who'd taken an interest, and as he made his way through school, they helped him "navigate through the insanity that is night school." He was working by day, in college at night. And despite the fact that it was a "tough road," there was a path, and he had a plan. The process of taking "slow, methodical" steps toward a goal, something that he'd learned and perfected at the dojo, had given him the experience of endurance. On what would become a pivotal night during this period in his life, when an unforeseen blow to the face would leave him on the pavement, Tim had a year and a half of college under his belt. He'd been gaining traction.

Vinnie was a "New York cop," Tim recalls. Tough, big, and very accomplished in martial arts. When he took you into the dojo, he meant to knock you around a bit. And the day that Sensei put Tim on the floor with Vinnie was no different. Since the attack, Tim had been teetering, on the brink of "leaving everything behind." The question whirring around in his head, overcoming his hope for the future, was "What else is going to come along to knock you away from school, or knock you away from a job?" But as they sparred, Vinnie asked different questions: Could I have done anything? Could Sensei? Tim had to answer no. And then, it was like an "instant switch," he reports. The self-interrogation stopped.

Although damaging, the assault "was a circumstance, it was something that happened, and I had beaten circumstance before," Tim shares. In that context, the incident lost its grip.

Tim would go on to write a book on personal safety and dedicate it to Sensei Sara. In keeping with her teachings of a "payback type of philosophy," he donated proceeds to an organization that worked with survivors of violence, turning the horror of that night into a "circle around." He also went on to teach martial arts to kids, taking to heart Sensei's instruction that success was not just for oneself. "As you grew up in the ranks, you had more responsibility to actually help others," Tim recalls. And after completing night school, he made his way into the professional world, initially at smaller companies and then, landing a global role to which he'd aspired. The first time he applied for that position, the interviewer rejected him, saying that he didn't have the right qualifications. Upon reapplying when the position became vacant again a couple of years later, he was met by the same interviewer. This time, he pressed and suggested that he was capable. In the end, he got the job and the thanks of a grateful employer. That role was the beginning of a career working across the globe, authoring more books and articles, and helping others progress in their own careers. I tell him during our interview that it strikes me as gutsy to not only reapply but also face the person who'd already once disqualified him. Tim tells me that in his head he'd been thinking, "Maybe you're playing at a black belt level, and right now I'm a green belt. . . . What else do I need to do? You tell me."

Given the challenges he'd overcome, it's hard to imagine that Tim might look back and think that he'd do anything differently at all, but he shares with me that there is one thing he wished he'd gotten earlier, understood sooner. "The tough things that you have, whether it's in life or work or family . . . let it pass if they're those uncontrollable things," he reflects. There were times growing up when he was annoyed and frustrated at situations in his life that were not in his power to change, and for those that were particularly tough, he relays that he "didn't realize how heavy anger was." It was much later before he realized that not only was he lighter without it but also that not carrying it made his own progress easier, as well as his work "lifting other people up."

In part, Tim's story is an extraordinary account about the lens we look through and its power to shape the course of our lives. But it is also a narrative about a vision holder who altered the course of Tim's trajectory by helping him see when he could not. As critical as our frame of reference is, it is not enough. We need others along the way. And perhaps those who are the most complete vision holders do more than see our potential and nourish it. Instead, they also steadfastly accompany us, when we're not soaring, when there has been a significant setback, or, as was the case for Tim, when we are in danger of utter derailment, and in those times, help us find our way back to ourselves so that we might find our way forward again.

As he looks back on that 12-year-old kid who was taken in by a sensei, Tim tells me that he was "really lucky." I can't help but think of the contrast between the boy who couldn't see a viable path out of the neighborhood and the man whose frame of reference is "Know your circumstances, find a work-around from it, and then get really methodical about moving to the next step." We can't know what might have become of his life's arc had Tim not wandered into that martial arts school, nor can we know what might have happened had he walked away from his new life when he was struggling to recover after the attack. But it's likely not an exaggeration to suggest that the second juncture was as critical as the first and that had his teacher not known her student, not known that he was in trouble, some, if not all, of the accomplishment of Tim's life since might have evaporated into an unfollowed future.

Tim tells me that they are still in touch.

And that he still calls her Sensei Sara.

CHAPTER 5

Undaunted: Stretching Through Fear

Featured Narrative: Carolyn Colvin, Former Acting Commissioner, Social Security Administration

You never know all you need to know for any of life's experience.

Sometimes an arc in life becomes a circle, a single point both launch and return. For Carolyn Colvin, that place was the Social Security Administration. As a young working woman, she began as a typist and later returned to become deputy commissioner at the request of President Obama, coming out of retirement to lead the organization of 65,000. For "a little girl who grew up in a two bedroom home, without inside plumbing," she says, "it was the highest honor."

"But," she adds, "for every job that I've taken, I've been scared to death."

It is this matter-of-fact disclosure and lack of pretense during our interview that give me a window into the sincerity and humanity that infuse Carolyn Colvin. Guided by her mother's values and expectations, the person she describes as her "greatest inspiration," I get the sense that although Carolyn has traveled a great distance from her start in life, she remains grounded by its circumstances and her mother's influence, allowing their imprint to guide her work in public service.

One of 14 children, Carolyn Colvin's mother left grade school to take care of her younger siblings, using the Bible and newspaper to educate herself. She worked in low-paying domestic jobs, as a childcare provider, often using the opportunity of a trip to the library to learn, herself. Later, she'd take pride in beating Carolyn and her sister, both college educated, in games of Scrabble. She imparted values of integrity and "the importance of giving back." Finding a coin in the street meant donating it to the church. And Carolyn knew that when she was out in the world, she carried the honor of the family name with her, was its representative. Despite having passed away several years ago, Carolyn's mother still serves as both touchstone and beacon for this leader of one of the great institutions of the United States. Reflecting over her life and career, Carolyn says of her mother, "I've tried to live a life that you would have been proud of."

Initially determined to work in education, believing, as her mother did, that education was the means by which people could affect their station in life, Carolyn changed direction early on while working in a hospital. She saw firsthand the "disparity" between how people with means were treated versus those without. And it was that close-up view that caused her to pursue a broader focus for her career, to invest her efforts in an even bigger lever than education. She realized that "it was really government that determined how you live and how you die, and I wanted to be certain that I had some ability to influence that. Public service was the answer."

Driven by a passion and purpose so intertwined as to make them indistinguishable from one another, Carolyn was committed to making "a significant difference in the lives of people," she tells me. And in so doing, she was simultaneously revolutionizing the course of her own trajectory. Working three jobs while raising her two boys on her own, she attended college, constrained only by the number of free evenings her rigorous work schedule would permit. It would be 14 years of night school before she earned her degree. And it is here in our conversation that I ask if things ever seemed bleak.

"It was not easy," she says without a trace of self-pity. Sure, there were times when she felt overwhelmed, wondering if she'd cross the finish line. But Carolyn was the inaugural member of her family to attend college and carried its significance not only for herself but for those who had been rooting for her. Scores of family members, all without means themselves, contributed whatever they could, often only "nickels and dimes." And so, even when it was a struggle, the import and weight of her efforts were sustaining: "I felt that I needed to be successful for myself as well as for them," she shares.

Carolyn went on to serve as she envisioned, working in public sector positions in Maryland and Washington, DC, even spending several years at the Social Security Administration during the 1990s in different roles. There were a couple of years spent as the CEO of Amerigroup Community Care before becoming special assistant to the secretary of the Maryland Department of Transportation in 2009. And, then, the call from the White House. In 2010, she was asked to serve as the deputy commissioner of the Social Security Administration, a request that she describes as "the highlight of my career." She returned to lead the organization where she began as that young typist, an institution that had personally touched her life and the lives of those she loves. She'd seen how Social Security was there for her four young grandchildren when her son passed away at age 34. She knew the safety net it provided, its critical impact. She'd watched the elders in her community, including her own mother, rely on its earned benefit. She had witnessed that it was "the most important social program that this country has ever developed." After becoming deputy commissioner, she later served as acting commissioner, leading the entire organization. The point of launch and return was also pinnacle.

Carolyn may have experienced trepidation when taking on new roles, but she seems to have an instinctual bent toward leadership that many leaders struggle to adopt their entire careers. As we delve into the intricacies of shepherding the Social Security Administration, she talks about encouraging innovation and about how crucial a leader's response is "when something doesn't quite go as planned." In that moment, leaders set the tone for all future innovation, she says, and if employees think "they're going to get in trouble," it will forever inhibit their risk-taking. We talk, too, about getting buy-in from stakeholders, and she admits to walking into meetings knowing "exactly what I wanted to do" and coming out "going in a totally different direction because I'd listened to employees, heard what they had to say, realized that there were things I hadn't considered." She knew she wanted to establish multiple channels of communication from the front lines of the organization to its senior leadership, and created, among other vehicles, virtual town hall meetings where she and 20,000 of her staff could interact.

And what about leading the leader? When I ask Carolyn about passion's role in the work of leadership, if it affects leadership performance, it's as if I've inquired if giraffes are tall. "Oh my goodness!" she exclaims. "You must have passion." Simply put, the challenges are too great. We go on to discuss the demands of leading an organization of that stature and size, of having multiple bosses, including Congress, about "being pulled in so many directions," of staying focused on the priority and mission of the organization, and of "getting the right benefits to the right people at the right time."

If Carolyn Colvin has a leadership credo, it might be captured by her suggestion that leaders not take credit for achievements. "You want to let their light sort of shine through you," she says of employees. It's this poetic vision of leadership that makes me wonder if her dedication to working in public service contends for first place in her heart with the work of developing others. Because, when she was a young woman setting out on her path, Carolyn looked forward and pledged her efforts to those institutions serving this country's most vulnerable. And, now, at 74, having traveled that journey, glancing back, she shares that what fills her with the most pride is "the emerging leaders that I developed who are going to be able to take the organization into the next century."

Considering the person who was her life's second greatest influence, Carolyn's desire to grow and groom other leaders should not come as a surprise. Governor Schaefer of Maryland was the person who translated her mother's teachings into the formal work of public service, the person who guided her in applying those values to an organizational context, when she first worked for him while he was the mayor of Baltimore City. "He taught us, he expected us, to serve people and to really focus on the one person who was before us," she explains. But at the same time the governor was demonstrating what it was to lead an organization, he was also modeling what it meant to lead its people. "Governor Donald Schaefer believed that if he saw an ounce of potential, that he wanted you on his team," Carolyn says. During our interview, it is clear the baton has been passed. As we talk about the essence of leadership and what it means to her, Carolyn says with utter conviction that it is "helping people to see what they are capable of."

It would seem that life's struggles have not tempered Carolyn Colvin's optimism but informed it. When I ask if her leadership of self relates to leading an organization, there seems to be a natural confluence between the bravery and perseverance of her personal journey and the enormous responsibility and vision of guiding an organization:

> On the journey, you're going to sometimes move away from the direction in which you thought you were going. You may have a lot of turnarounds. You're going to have detours in your life. But if you have a real purpose, or a real desire, you'll figure out a different path of how to get you there.

CHAPTER 6

Focusing on Success While Remaining Open to Iteration

Featured Narrative: Tom O'Keefe, Actor, Bedlam Theater Company

I'm not putting an end date on when I'm going to think I've achieved success.

REM's song *This Could Be the Saddest Dusk* was playing on Tom O'Keefe's Walkman as he made his way to the mailbox. On lunch break from his summer internship at the attorney general's office in Massachusetts, he was thinking about what he'd tell his father, the man who'd poured equal amounts of tuition and pride into his son's future as an attorney. The last of six children, Tom knew the cost of attending Boston University's law school. He'd seen how hard his parents had worked to attain their financial security, how they'd started out with nothing. And as he took the T back to his apartment that day, he was panicked. Grades were in. Despite the nightmares he'd been having about exams, he'd liked the first year of law school, the rigor of studying. Criminal law was particularly appealing for its rhetoric and drama and the opportunity to be in the courtroom. But if he'd flunked his criminal law exam, he was decided: He'd let go of becoming a prosecutor, a U.S. attorney, and quit law school to become an actor. Bracing himself, he opened the envelope and started to laugh. He'd gotten the highest score in the class.

"Well," he thought, staring down, incredulous, "this is what I'm supposed to do. I'm supposed to be a lawyer." That first year, Tom received the Book Award for his highest grade and finished number two in his class overall. At the end of his three years in law school, a hair separated him from graduating summa cum laude, finishing, as he did, among the top 10 students out of approximately 350. He took the distinction of magna cum laude with him to the associate job waiting at the Boston law firm of Goodwin, Procter, and Hoar. He'd worked there as a summer associate after finishing his second year. That same year, while fielding multiple offers from big firms, he joined a band as its lead singer. It was also the year he'd had a failed audition for Legal Follies, the group at Boston University that put on an annual variety show. Before his third year of law school was complete, he had an offer from Goodwin.

He'd chosen Goodwin because, he tells me, "It seemed the best of all worlds." Not only was it a "respected firm with great people doing some great corporate litigation work," but a number of the firm's lawyers were former U.S. attorneys, including two of Tom's mentors. The firm had a program with the Middlesex District Attorneys (DA's) office where they'd send a couple of second-year associates to work for six months while still collecting their salaries from Goodwin. It was, Tom remembers, "a good way to make money, get experience, make connections, and then move on and become a US attorney, if that was still my dream." More than a decade would pass before he would make "the very distinct connection between lawyering and Shakespeare" and a couple of years after that when he would be in rehearsals for a production of Hamlet in New York City.

Tom first considered the notion "to take on acting" in high school. He'd auditioned and performed in a few shows. At that time, there was also the "side note" of considering the Air Force Academy. Participating in band, rather than acting, was likely a better fit for the Air Force track. But, as the next step toward his future came into focus, Tom recalls, "In the end, it was to go to college and become a lawyer." During college, there were a handful of acting classes, the thought to add theater as a minor, and the Shakespeare class where the words were spoken aloud and he was utterly captivated. But law school would not only provide him with the "financial stability" that he'd seen his parents valiantly achieve, but Tom thought, "That's the career path that fits me." When we look back together during our interview and I ask him about that time, he doesn't recall wondering about what he'd do. "To be honest," he says, "I didn't really struggle with it."

At Goodwin, he was hardly miserable as an attorney. Was acting knocking at all, I want to know? Was it whispering? "I don't recall thinking about it," Tom tells me in all candor. He was working, fulfilling his "dream of becoming a prosecutor." But then, what came next was "really wacky," he remembers. His girlfriend had gone to a tarot card reader. She called Tom afterward to report that when the reader discovered that Tom was an attorney, the tarot reader blurted out, "How dare he!" Looking back, Tom says that reaction could have meant any number of things. Perhaps the tarot card reader had been sued or had an ex-husband who was an attorney. Or just hated lawyers. But when Tom heard those words, he blurted out in response, "Yeah, I should be acting."

Despite the just-below-the surface immediacy of his response, what followed could best be described as "gradual with stutter steps and lots of tripping," he tells me. No sooner did he get off the phone with his girlfriend than Tom did an Internet search and e-mailed an acting school in California. He gave them a sketch: Twenty-eight years old and an attorney, he'd acted a bit in high school and college and wanted their suggestions. Within an hour, a response. The school was holding an intensive seminar the following weekend. In Boston. He shares with me that while he "had a good time with it," he didn't make any big changes to his life.

But he was taking steps. At the conclusion of the weekend intensive, the instructors pulled him aside. "You have something," they said. Those words at that juncture. They provided some reassurance, some reflection. "This passion of mine that's been hidden away and keeps popping up at the interesting moments," he recalls thinking, "is grounded in some reality." He'd needed that. Because wrapped around the pursuit of acting were a series of strung-together questions that plagued him: "Should I really be doing this, or is this just ego? Who do I think I am? Am I fooling myself?" That nod toward his talent prodded him to further action, nudged him along. He took a few more acting classes near Boston. He remained at Goodwin but downsized from his solo one bedroom to sharing an apartment with a roommate to save money. He was looking into acting, dipping a toe in the water, but wasn't about to plunge in full-time.

But now, at this place, there is "something of a struggle," Tom recalls. He was toggling, caught between "am I going to do this, am I not?" He had one foot each in two worlds. And he remained in that place of back and forth for almost two years. The world of the law had its prescribed track, a well-marked route. And, while not guaranteed, the hard work it demanded likely granted ascension. That path came with "its set of accolades or respect in traditional society." It was acceptable. The world of acting, however, only promised to fulfill his passion. He knew one thing: If he did it, he would go to Los Angeles (LA). New York, while closer and likely a very good place to begin acting, was dangerous. It would put him in the same city where Goodwin had a branch office. He would be in proximity to family in nearby Connecticut. The next step would have to be big, he knew. It would have been easy to just "give up acting and go back to my job," he remembers. Reflecting during our interview, Tom's relays that "the only thing that was getting in my way" was how unsure acting was. But there was more. There was the practical. It wasn't as if he had a map for launching an acting career. "How do I do it?" was another hesitation. And, then, perhaps the question that held his greatest reluctance: "How do I tell my Dad?"

It would be Tom's father who would inform his son that it was time. Still at Goodwin, Tom had a week's vacation planned for LA. With friends living there, the idea was to go "just to look around" and continue his inch-by-inch exploration of acting. But he did not make that trip. Instead, he flew home to be with his mother who was dying. A woman who'd once wanted to act, herself, Tom recalls a moment between them when she was still lucid, before the Alzheimer's made her seriously ill. He'd shared what he was considering and she shared her cautious excitement for him. A week after her death, Tom's toggling ceased and the struggle was over. With his father's blessing and gentle push, he returned to Boston, to Goodwin, and as colleagues were offering their condolences, he walked into the office of the partners, closed the door, and offered his resignation. He was leaving for Los Angeles. For acting.

With the savings he'd socked away, Tom felt confident that he could sustain himself for two years while he attempted to get himself established. And it would be that long before he began booking commercials. But he found opportunity in LA. There would be at least one national spot in commercials each year, even some guest spots on TV. While he hadn't found extraordinary success, and there were times when he didn't have work, he'd gained a foothold. But after almost 10 years in LA, something eluded him. He'd begun to feel "stagnant." Despite the hard work and reward of launching his acting career, he "wasn't feeling really fulfilled." Most of his time was spent auditioning for commercials or preparing to audition. He was doing one play a year, at most. "I wasn't spending my daily life as an actor," Tom explains to me.

Performing a scene from Tennessee Williams's *Orpheus Descending* would change that. On stage during a weeklong intensive class, Tom was instantly reunited with why he'd gone to LA in the first place. "This is why I became an actor," he recalls thinking. Theater. He went home to find his copy of *King Lear*. Reading it again, he was transported back to the college class where he'd first been "so moved" by Shakespeare, by hearing it read aloud. At that moment, he knew: "That's the stuff that I want to do." It would be New York, after all. But not before immersing himself in classical theater.

Leaving LA, Tom focused on Shakespeare. He sought out training at weekend intensives, spent time at the theater company of Shakespeare and Company, and worked in plays throughout New England, practicing his craft. Law school, it turned out, had not been in vain, had not been an error. Despite the difficulty often associated with its first year, he'd had a passion for learning the cases and discovered a "real love for rhetoric, for words, for using the right words." During his first weekend Shakespeare intensive after leaving LA, he saw it. Law school, with its emphasis on argument and word precision, had not only been excellent training for reciting and performing Shakespeare, it made perfect sense.

After a year of "living like a nomad," of going from play to play to learn and train, it was finally time for New York. But arriving "was kind of like a slap in the face," Tom tells me. The promise of doing great work might have been waiting, but so was a New York winter. And the fact that he knew no one. And that no one knew him. It was demoralizing that he needed to find an apartment with a roommate at that stage in his life. He was starting over again. And "starting over much older," he emphasizes. The first year in New York he characterizes as "very rough." In darker moments, the questions came: "Why did I become an actor to begin with? This is just silly. Why didn't I just stay in LA? I was making a living."

This second leap was more difficult than when he set out for LA. It asked that he relinquish the success in LA to embark on another route that once again had no defined guideposts or markers. It required that he confront that he "still had the mindset of being someone who is on the traditional path" and attempt to let go of it, at least temporarily. Even if he hadn't been performing theater in LA, at least, Tom relays, "I had been making money on commercials, so it was easy to call myself an actor." In New York, he was redefining what it meant to be an actor. "It sounds a little pretentious to me," he relays, "but I have to convince myself that it's the work that's the most important." New York asked a lot. But there was a cadre of support: his dad, a sister in nearby Connecticut, and dear friends from law school and childhood he calls "bedrocks." All provided infusions of encouragement and sustenance.

As Tom tells me about beginning all over again, I wonder if Los Angeles, like law school, wasn't a fundamental and necessary step toward performing classical theater, rather than a warm-up or derailment. I wonder if for him to get to New York, he had to go to LA and succeed for almost 10 years to then discern that it wasn't merely acting that he wanted, but Shakespeare. And, I wonder if his ability to leap, not once but twice, exemplifies a seemingly contrasting, yet essential, merging of two ingredients necessary for full prosperity: a deep and fixed determination for success with an openness to what presents itself, to iteration.

Temporarily setting aside material gain was, Tom tells me, "one of the more difficult things" for him during this time. I ask if he was able to change his perspective on New York and starting over. And if so, how? "I started doing plays and feeling like I was doing the right work," he says. He was working with people he admired, doing the kind of theater he'd yearned for. One thing led to another. At the time of our interview, Tom had been in New York for two years. He was "deep in rehearsals" for Bedlam Theater Company's second production, Shakespeare's *Hamlet*. The year before, he'd performed in their inaugural show, George Bernard Shaw's *Saint Joan*. Bedlam was brand new to the New York theater scene, a start-up, and a "tiny, little theater company with no money" launched by two friends he met during his time spent studying theater in the year between LA and New York. *Saint Joan*, a play in which "every scene is an argument," drew on Tom's love of law school. Brought in as one of four actors in the production, he played 11 of the 25 characters. There were frequent character changes, often without costume, in the span of a few minutes. It was risky. He worried if the audience would buy it.

The contrast between working in New York and LA was not lost on Tom. At the time of our interview, he had fulfilled his reason for moving to New York, to focus "mainly on theater" and found himself a combination of happy and exhausted. Time spent in LA auditioning for commercials had been replaced by rehearsals for Bedlam's follow-up to *Saint Joan*, with a few actors taking on many different parts once again in *Hamlet*. Rehearsals typically ran 8 to 10 hours a day. "At last count," he tells me, "I'm playing nine characters." He is finally on stage, finally with Shakespeare. How was *Saint Joan* received, I want to know? "It was really kind of comforting," he says candidly. *The New York Times* named it a Critics' Pick. *The Wall Street Journal* praised it as the best revival of the year. And the most exciting revival ever.

CHAPTER 7

Questing for Self-Mastery

Featured Narrative: Logan Bennett, President of the Alberta Avalanche Rescue Dog Association, Director of the Canadian Avalanche Rescue Dog Association, and Avalanche Forecaster/Assistant Supervisor of Snow Safety at Sunshine Village Ski Resort

It was a big avalanche, it was size 2, big enough to bury a person. And it had totally surprised me.

When buried under snow, human scent emanates as a "cone-like feature" Logan Bennet tells me. Ferra's job is to locate that cone. And then start digging. Golden-hued and small for a German shepherd, Ferra is Logan's partner in their work of avalanche rescue, mobilizing to search for buried skiers after an unexpected avalanche. When they're not searching, Logan works as an avalanche forecaster and is the assistant supervisor of snow safety at Sunshine Village ski resort in the Canadian Rockies. Working primarily in avalanche mitigation, he creates controlled avalanches to make the slopes safer for skiers.

Using a technique called ski cutting, Logan will "weight the slope" with his own body, skiing across the terrain, deliberately causing it to release and creating an avalanche. Avalanches are classified as sizes 1 to 5 and those that Logan creates with ski cutting go up to 1.5 and are "not harmful to humans." Size 2, however, will bury a person. And on a routine day of ski cutting, after working a slope for hours, preparing it for a controlled release, Logan was fighting to stay upright as a size 2 avalanche took him down a mountain. Had he been buried, his own dog, Ferra, would have been used to search for him.

The first time Logan Bennett was on skis, he fell in love. Seven years old, his dad took him out on the slopes of their native New Zealand, and he became enamored, hook, line, and sinker. When he went off to college at Canterbury University, it was to study geology, and he kept himself on the slopes working as a part-time ski patroller at Temple Basin lodge, delivering first aid to injured skiers. But after a close friend committed suicide, Logan reevaluated his career path in geology and decided to go full-time as a ski patroller. He knew, "I just wanted to ski; that's all I ever wanted to do." The day he was caught in a size 2 avalanche, he'd been doing avalanche mitigation work since 1998. Almost 20 years.

"Snow," Logan explains, is "basically made up of layers, and you'll often have a layer that's more problematic." It's those weaker layers, "under the snow, that the avalanche can release on," he says. Logan and his partner had gone out to open and prepare a slope for skiers. It was one that Logan personally loved, "a really great area" that he frequently skied, and he "really wanted to open it for everyone else." Opening this particular area was tricky. The challenge was the "very fine line" between leaving enough snow on the slope, particularly in the tightest part of the chute, and being able to "mitigate the hazard, in other words, cause the avalanche, but not so that it would ruin where we ski." So he and his partner went about "working the terrain," ski cutting while moving quickly and carefully between designated safe areas on the slope, wanting to get the snow just right. And he thought they had.

Had things gone as planned that day, only the slope on the far side would have released, and both Logan and his partner would have been well out of harm's way. But as Logan crossed over the slope to confirm that the far side was gone, he twisted around to signal to his partner and felt the entirety of what was beneath him start to move. Still carrying forward on his skis, he looked up to see the crown wall, about 80 feet above. The huge slab of snow that he was on had separated and broken free. An avalanche had initiated.

Fighting to stay on his feet, he was being taken down the mountain. The slab of snow had released at a weakened layer, all the way at "the bottom of the snow pack," and it was moving with increasing speed. There were pieces breaking off above, at the crown wall, raining down on him. And even though he was "still traversing at this point quite quickly" he was looking for a way out, looking for safety. And that's when he saw the tree. Diving and throwing himself onto it, he "clung to it quite heavily" as the avalanche continued and the entire slab of snow between him and the crown wall slid down the mountain, going through mature timber. To this day, he gives thanks to that tree "every time" he goes by.

When the avalanche was over, Logan immediately looked for his partner. Glancing over at the safe spot where he'd last been standing, Logan saw that he was no longer there. Calling on the radio yielded nothing and so, "quite worried," Logan set out to go look for him. And then he heard his partner's voice on the radio. The avalanche "had gone much wider than both of us had anticipated it could go, and much, much deeper," Logan says. Despite having been standing on a safe point, his partner had been swept off his feet. And pulled into the avalanche. It was a small tree that saved him, grabbing it as the snow dragged him by, swinging himself up and out of the avalanche as it barreled down the slope.

In the world of avalanche mitigation and snow science, there is a term for the "tendency to ignore people who don't have as much experience." It's called a "halo bias," Logan tells me. And he seems determined to avoid it. Despite his tremendous depth and breadth of experience and the "really humbling thing" of being caught unawares, and despite the comfort of knowing that he was surrounded by top-notch avalanche professionals who would be immediately dispatched if the situation were to become "really dire," Logan insists that the most important element of what happened that day is what transpired immediately afterward. After checking each other for injuries, he and his partner went back to the office and Logan convened the entire team, including his boss. He wanted to know two things: what had happened and why.

Snow science is not exact. Certainty is not possible. But on reflection, there were things that had been ignored. First, there had been a temperature spike that probably made the slab of snow more likely to be triggered. And, although Logan hadn't seen them, there had been other avalanches reported that day below tree line. And then there was his own desire to open the terrain and the fact that he was intimately acquainted with having "worked it a lot in the last 15 years." He was confident that he was making the right choice.

Hindsight may provide a type of clarity that is impossible to achieve real time, but Logan insists on looking back to see what he can learn for the future. And he wants to do it openly with his team so that they, too, will feel comfortable discussing their mistakes and then sharing that information with other avalanche professionals in the industry. Despite his vast experience, Logan understands that he is both leader and learner, that "no one is infallible," and that no one person can possibly have all the answers. To that end, he is committed to creating an environment where team members feel free to speak their mind, to share their ideas. He believes that this input from others makes him more "robust" as a leader, makes him better. He calls it "being supple and being ready to entertain other people's ideas." I ask him how leaders keep themselves open to other opinions when they already have so much experience and expertise to support their own thinking. Without hesitation, he says, "People who come in without any experience, they have one thing you don't have: They don't have your perspective." And when he and Ferra have been tasked to search for buried skiers after an unanticipated avalanche, it is this, the very presence of others' opinions, that gives him more confidence, not less, in the enormous responsibility of his search work with his dog.

Avalanche rescue, like snow science, is full of uncertainty. Sometimes people have been reported missing, and other times, it's Logan and Ferra, out in the avalanche debris, working and searching, their job to clear an area, to report that no one has been left. Tasked by Alberta Parks, Parks Canada, or, on occasion, the Royal Canadian Mounted Police, the canine-human unit of two is mobilized after the avalanche. Ideally, people who travel in avalanche terrain wear transceivers, but that's not always the case. And the next best thing, in Logan's opinion, is a dog's ability to search for scent. It requires that they work independently and in tandem with one another, flawlessly communicating, she searching and indicating to him, he watching and reading her. "It's important," Logan says, "that you have a really intimate relationship with your dog."

Arriving at a scene, Logan tries to locate a transceiver signal and Ferra tries to locate a scent. When she starts running in a pattern across the avalanche debris, Logan begins to watch her. Running through a scent, she'll catch it initially and then turn around to come back to it. In and out, in and out. A zigzagging Ferra gets Logan's attention; it means she's honing in on the scent cone. When she begins to aggressively dig, Logan will join her to probe for a subject. Digging is indicating. It means that spot, that very point "is the emanation of the scent from the snow."

They trained for two-and-a-half years together, for this, their work on the slopes of the Canadian Rockies, training with the search organization, the Canadian Avalanche Rescue Dog Association (CARDA), and then going for certification with the Royal Mounted Canadian Police, the validating body that certifies that they are prepared and able to do this work, every day, unfailingly. The work of training meant giving Ferra the skills of searching. It meant attending multiple, intensive spring and winter courses together, of teaching her, at the beginning, to search for him hiding with a piece of fabric in his hands to then searching for a piece of human-scented fabric buried under snow. Progress is made in increments. Things get harder. The fabric is buried deeper, in a bigger area. Dogs have to find it in less time. There are always setbacks. And, in the end, after more than two years of training, some dogs are not able to make the "mental leap" from searching for a live person to searching for a piece of fabric. Logan has seen instances where dogs and their handlers get "to these really critical stages" and the dog is unable to make the transition. There are mentors from CARDA available for the problems that will undoubtedly arise. On the day of the exam, buried 70 to 75 cm deep, somewhere in a 100-meter × 100-meter square on a slope, were three or four pieces of fabric with human scent on them. Logan did not know where they were. Ferra had to find them. Within 45 minutes.

But in addition to teaching Ferra to search, Logan had to teach himself about Ferra. He had to see and understand his dog. How did she best learn? How much training was too much before she'd tire? Or get bored? What would keep her so interested and excited that she'd keep going, keep searching for the fabric, keep working? His retired search dog Cai was able to tolerate training every day. Ferra had a different temperament, softer. And Logan knew that if he pushed her too hard, if he forced her to do more than she was ready to do, she would wilt. Despite always doing what he's asked of her, Logan has never "asked her to do something she's super-uncomfortable with." And when he introduces her to a new environment, one that will be challenging for her, he ensures that he does it "in a way with which that she won't be too stressed about it, that she can do it." They have built trust and understanding across the boundary of species. Logan knows that when the stakes are at their highest, Ferra is capable of finding someone buried in the snow. And Ferra knows that Logan will ask her to learn and to work, but he will not push her to her detriment. Even still, with all the training hours the two have logged, with a partnership built solidly on a foundation of trust, and with being tested, the two of them, repeatedly, under duress, there is still more to understand and to learn. There is the skill, yes, and the practice, but there is also the fundamental desire to continue to strengthen his relationship with the partner he also refers to as his best friend. "Getting to know your dog is really a journey in itself," Logan says.

And yet, despite the intensive training with Ferra and returning for certification every year to stay at "peak level," even with mentorship, and the years of experience, there remains the tremendous weight of responsibility in an avalanche search, to say that no one has been left, and making that call as accurately as possible while minimizing time on the slopes and the risk to the rescue teams. There is the stress of the "what if" scenarios that run through Logan's mind. What if the scent conditions were bad? What if someone is buried? Left?

Ski cutting mitigates avalanche risk. And there are two elements of leadership that seem to mitigate the fears and pressures likely intrinsic to that work. First, Logan is committed to self-mastery, to "never stop learning." And he is equally dedicated to being an evergreen student with Ferra. "I'm constantly learning on the things that I can improve with my dog to make her better and us a better team," he says. The sharper his ability to read her and receive what she is communicating, the stronger they are together. And even though he is the president of the Alberta Avalanche Rescue Dog Association, the fundraising and outfitting organization for handlers and their dogs for the entire province, Logan is resolute in his own search: to know and digest more, to always be improving.

Second, he relies on, and has confidence in, the team of avalanche professionals that he has built and nurtured. He knows that when decisions are being made to put teams on the slopes after an avalanche, when circumstances dictate the very highest level of expertise of everyone in the room, Logan's got it. And his team knows that if any one of them thinks that an unproductive search might have missed something, they'll go back out. They know that, in Logan's words, "no opinion is invalid." Under these, the highest of stakes, he knows that he has the best thinking and experience in the room, and that his is, literally, an informed decision.

Featured Narrative: Brad Wilson, President and CEO, Blue Cross Blue Shield of North Carolina

If you look at any revolution that's ever occurred in history, when the revolution happens, there's fear, there's uncertainty, there are voids that need to be filled . . . and guess who fills them? Leaders.

Brad Wilson of Blue Cross Blue Shield of North Carolina has been steering the eight-billion-dollar insurance organization through the tumult of U.S. health care since he became its CEO in 2010. A liberal arts major, his path to the top might be called unusual. He doesn't have an MBA and instead holds a JD and a graduate degree in liberal studies. When he talks about leading through uncertainty, he quotes Napoleon. And his advice to young people aspiring to carve a similar ascension to CEO? Become a Renaissance person.

Sometime during the third grade, Brad Wilson discovered biographies and in so doing, inadvertently began his education as CEO, one that he would return to and rely on over and over again. But that was to come much later. His boyhood interest in history followed him to college at Appalachian State University in the mountains of North Carolina, where he made it his major, and philosophy his minor. From there, it was on to law school at Wake Forest University, a route inspired, in many ways, by all the biographies he'd digested. So many of those people had been lawyers, and it was a career that, in Brad's estimation, positioned them to "make a positive contribution," no matter what they did.

While he was soaking up the pages of history during his early years, he was also absorbing the lessons imparted by his father and high school football coach, two men who would shape his development and who "contributed in an extraordinary way to the grounding" that Brad describes as both bedrock and guide for how he leads himself and his organization. His father showed him what it was to use one's talents and abilities to live in such a way as to "make life better, for somebody, somewhere." It was instruction by action, rather than mere words, and Brad says that he "could see it" in how his father lived his own life. Of his high school football coach, Brad says, "He taught me that I could always perform better than I thought, that I could play above my ability." One man showed him how to use his capabilities in the world, the other showed him what it was to stretch beyond them. Both he credits with instilling the fundamentals of right and wrong, the beliefs about how one should live and behave, and, ultimately, about who one is. And both taught him how to lose.

I wonder how this knowledge of history combines with the lessons from his childhood to influence Brad in the present day. It seems that as much as he is a student of historical events, Brad is also a student of the leaders who shaped them. He's spent time considering their common behaviors and processes, particularly under difficult circumstances. He's tried to, as he describes it, "distill out the lessons that can be applied universally" to what he's facing in the here and now, lessons about character, about inspiring followers, about carrying the burdens of leadership and the pressures of making difficult decisions, and about the role of leadership, itself.

"Every leader faces complex situations, but it's not like Harry Truman having to decide whether or not and when to drop the atomic bomb on Japan," Brad tells me. We've been talking about the context that history lends itself to, to the perspective that it gives him in the midst of leading through the high stakes of change and tumult. U.S. health care has been undergoing a transformation, Brad explains, and with the signing of the Affordable Care Act in 2010, "An emerging revolution was accelerated." With it, so, too, was uncertainty and the critical importance of leading himself and his organization through it. He does not shy away from the challenges of complexity or making decisions under those conditions, but history has granted him a vantage point to crisis and challenge that has enabled him to develop a resilience and perspective for evaluating the most complex situations. Reflecting on the past, he says, "When you think the burdens that you are carrying are too heavy for you to bear, remembering that there have been many others that have had far more complex circumstances, kind of helps you keep your head about you." And it is from here, looking through this lens, that Brad is able to draw on the tools he's come to understand that make for skilled decision-making.

History tells him the importance of setting priorities and setting them in order. But history also reveals that "life is not linear, that it's very complex and that you need to listen and look broadly, you need to be deliberate and not rush to judgment," he says. He knows that even when the pressure is on, even when the challenge great, perhaps even more so during those circumstances, "The prism of decision-making needs to be turned many times in all of the angles of light." Change and uncertainty might be accelerating, but decisions, Brad has come to understand, must be well considered. So how does he not rush to judgment when the challenge is great and the stakes high? For one, he's constructed a "24-hour rule" that he invokes whenever possible, one where he self-imposes a moratorium on making a final decision. There are situations when even 24 hours cannot be reserved for further deliberation so immediate is the decision, but whenever it is available to him, Brad doesn't "take any action for at least 24 hours." Rarely, he says, is there a major course correction on an original decision, but sometimes, there is a "ten-fifteen degree dial right or left."

He also knows that before he ever gets to the final stage of a decision, the light dispersed through that prism contains the full spectrum of opinion from colleagues around him. Like Logan Bennett, Brad is committed to getting all available information from his team and knows that it ultimately makes him better at what he does, better for Blue Cross. He recalls that great historical figures like Lincoln deliberately built their cabinets to include dissenting voices. And Brad doesn't want "just a little bit" of opinion and dissent, he emphasizes, he wants it all, and in an "unvarnished way." But fully eliciting it was considerably more difficult than he originally thought when he became CEO. In fact, it almost escaped him.

After law school, Brad served in Governor Jim Hunt's administration as his general counsel. And, later, he walked through the doors of Blue Cross Blue Shield to work there in the same capacity. Then, promoted from within Blue Cross, he rose to CEO from among a team that was already in place, already functioning well. And he assumed that just because he was in a different seat, the "clarity of dissent" he'd receive wouldn't change. He was the same person, after all, and these were his colleagues with whom he'd always shared the free flow of information. But he was mistaken. His seat made all the difference. Sitting at the head of the table, it turned out, "had a larger impact that I would ever have anticipated," Brad remembers. He came to understand that he not only had to reassure his colleagues that he wanted their dissent, he also had to demonstrate it. "Because of the mantle of your authority, you can shut down the conversation or you can turn the spigot down so that what you're getting is a trickle rather than the full flood of information," he stresses. He had to do more than give permission for dissent, he had to give the clear message that it was expected, even rewarded. Emphasizing the importance of creating a "safe environment," one in which people feel free and comfortable to speak up, Brad explains that his own behavior was one of the key building blocks for that container, highlighting the importance of "being self-aware, trying to be steady, not overreact." In other words, his ability to lead others was contingent upon his skill at leading himself.

No matter how helpful the lessons of the past for leading his organization, or how much he might wish to apply them, they would all be for naught if Brad were unable to first lead himself. If he were not committed to self-mastery, to continuing to stretch and constantly improve, he likely wouldn't be as effective or able to execute, as able to guide Blue Cross through the choppy waters and into the future with success. He is unequivocal: "You can't have positive business results without effective leadership." But he also knows that equally important, and an integral part of leadership's self-mastery, is not just the outward stretch toward more knowledge and learning but also the inner knowing of when he's stretched too thin, himself.

It's no secret that the pressures of executive leadership are none too gentle, the situations incredibly complex and challenging, the decisions high stakes. How does Brad steer himself under those circumstances, I want to know? How does he self-lead within that vice grip? He shares that there are times when he's found himself having "drifted away" from what he knows is his bedrock foundation, those values and guiding principles instilled in his youth. He's experienced "feeling alone or out of control" in leadership's ocean, he says. But he knows how to find his way back to shore, to that solid foundation instilled during his youth. And in addition to the team that surrounds him, the one that he's deliberately imbued with the mandate to, what he calls, "speak truth to power," he relies on his wife of 40 years and good friends to help him recognize when he might be off-kilter. When he finds himself pulled ever farther from himself, he draws on an assemblage of internal resources to get himself "righted," as he describes it.

The very first thing he does is nothing. Externally, if at all possible, he invokes his 24-hour rule, slowing a final decision, buying time, he says, to "sleep on it." And internally, within himself, he slows things, as well. Enunciating slowly and with great emphasis, Brad tells me that "quiet time alone" is his first go-to for righting himself. He steps away from the "clutter of the moment," from its cacophony, to seek space and "time for reflection," a place he describes as somewhere where one "can literally, mentally and physically, settle your emotions, your well-being." From this place of solitude and quiet, Brad says he is able to gather his thoughts and return to being "centered and grounded." From this firm footing, he is then able to make decisions with the clarity of his guiding principles. From this place of solidity, he knows that if he does turn the decision dial post-moratorium, it is calibrated against the knowing of what he believes, the foundation of right and wrong established as a boy, learned from watching his father.

That fundamental bedrock is also what informs his approach to leading his many "colleagues," as he calls the employees of Blue Cross. We've been talking about staying connected to employees and staying in front of them, about keeping his door open and being accessible. I want to know how he reconciles the time required to run his organization with his desire to cultivate real relationships with his employees. Like anything that's important, "You have to make it a priority," Brad explains. And once it's been made a priority, then it has to be carried out, action must be taken. It is here during our conversation, when we talk about how he relates to and leads the employees of Blue Cross, that he uses words like authenticity, vulnerability, and empathy. And talks about transparency, and not always having the answers. He describes the "Listening Tours" that he initiated to get in front of more employees, more often, traveling across the organization and country to different sites. There's no agenda for the block of 90 minutes; he has an open dialogue with whoever has signed up to attend. Attendance is capped at 30 for each session on the Tour, and officers of the company are not permitted to sign up. This is an opportunity for Brad to talk with employees at the front lines of the organization, and they to him. "Nothing's off limits," he says. After an initial 10 minutes of comments, he opens it up and "the floor is theirs." He may not have all the answers but is clear about one thing, and that's how he's going to show up: "It needs to be done authentically and genuinely. This is not a performance. It's a relationship," he says with certainty.

Not surprisingly, toward the end of our interview, as Brad looks back on the whole of his life and leadership experience to share his best advice gleaned from it, he again stresses the importance of creating relationships. Initially, when he proposes that a leader must be a "people person," I think he might be talking about the need to be gregarious or friendly, even. But as he fills in this description, I begin to see that the picture he's painting is one of a leader who retains a never-ending spirit of curiosity, however high the ascension. His suggestion? "All the time, in every walk of life, just simply get to know and learn from every person that you meet and continue to do that regardless of your vocation, station in life, title, family circumstance," he says. As he shares this wisdom, I wonder if he isn't simultaneously describing what lies at the heart of a Renaissance person as well as a leader who chooses the path of an ongoing quest for self-mastery: the essential belief that learning is infinite, as are its sources. And, I wonder, too, if that belief isn't best exemplified in Brad's simple but deeply held conviction that "there is a reservoir of knowledge and information and character everywhere."

CHAPTER 8

A Connection to Contribution: Creating a Footprint

Featured Narrative: Dana Born, Co-Director of the Center for Public Leadership at Harvard University's Kennedy School of Government, Lecturer in Public Policy, Retired Brigadier General, USAF, and Ninth Dean of the USAF Academy

There's a big focus on the crucible as a moment where we transition, I'll say, from "I" to "We."

Dana Born had a goal to climb all 55 of the 14,000+ foot peaks in Colorado, the state where she lived and worked as the ninth dean of the United States Air Force Academy. Only two peaks remained when she left for the East coast, for Harvard's Kennedy School of Government, where she would be teaching students and executives about leadership. A brigadier general who had a 30-year career in the USAF, who held positions of command during 9/11 and Afghanistan, Dana was retiring. Her family needed more of her attention, and there was a full bench of very capable leaders who could succeed her. If there was such a thing as an ideal time to leave, that was it. But the challenge, Dana tells me during our interview, was that in the military, "you get addicted to the mission." What would take its place? What could?

"It was a hard step," Dana recalls. The natural career move would have been to a university presidency, but that would have placed demands of time and social commitments on her family similar to those during her position as dean. And, besides, she wanted to give her full attention to transitioning well, to keeping it as smooth as possible for those whom she was leaving. Not to mention that it was a big move for her family; they'd been on the base in Colorado for 11 years. She'd tackle her next chapter a little later. But then the calls started coming in. She immediately ruled out the university presidencies that search firms brought. While she aspired to such a role in the future, it simply wasn't the right time, wasn't next. There was the nonprofit that was doing work in ethics and education that she explored. And then there was Harvard. It would mean being in the classroom again rather than administrating, and that was a huge draw. But it was the Kennedy School's mission, one that she describes as "developing top students for public service and preparing them to be successful in their passions to make the world a better place" that convinced her. It wasn't simply that the mission was so similar to the Academy's; it was that she thought it the place where she could bring her passion for leadership, for working with leaders of the future, to really make a difference.

"Having command is the pinnacle of being able to lead within our Air Force," Dana tells me. Earlier in her career, when she worked at the Pentagon on several policy assignments, a two-star general approached her to consider just such a position. And Dana's first response was to tell the general that her area was in policy. Command, Dana tells me, is a "huge responsibility and a great privilege," and one that she didn't feel ready for. Looking back, she says, "I didn't have the confidence that I had the ability because I hadn't had the experiences I thought you needed to be able to command." But when the general asked if she was declining, Dana could not. Her ascension to dean of the faculty was similar. There was a nudge from a mentor who asked if she was interested, and when Dana thought herself too junior for the role, her mentor suggested that Dana allow others to make that determination before disqualifying herself. In fact, it was Dana's duty to step forward to serve.

Reflecting back, there were many people "who believed more in me than I believed in myself," Dana recalls. People who had a profound influence on her life and career, who planted the seeds of ideas, made suggestions, saw her potential, helped her to see what was possible. She now measures her own success "to the extent that I'm able to do that for others," she tells me. Teaching at Harvard, being in the classroom "closer connected with students," as she describes it, was a way to do that.

Despite her successful path and the bounty of mentors, it wasn't always blue skies. Her own experiences with "crucible moments," as she calls them, times of trial for a leader, infuse the perspective she now brings to the classroom. "A real pivotal moment for me was a challenge I went through not long before I retired," Dana says. I've asked her about any critical junctures during her 30-year career and what might have helped her to steer through them. "Pivot points typically are around crucible moments, whether it's a failure or a death or a health challenge." But those times, as difficult as they are, can be used for reassessment and reevaluation of oneself, for taking stock of one's determination, focus, and direction. For Dana, that meant remembering where she most needed to invest her energy and attention, where it was most important. As Dean of the Faculty, "There were a lot of people that were relying on me to serve in that capacity and to stay focused on what it was that we were contributing to the overall mission," she recalls.

In her course on authentic leadership at Harvard, she teaches her students about the importance of crucibles, that the choices leaders make during those times of trial are not only about how they find their way through, but about what lies beyond, about how to use a particularly difficult circumstance for something more. She shares a snowboarding analogy with me and explains that snow boarders who are able to go quite high "are not always successful in terms of what they do at the top. Their success is really about how they transition through the lowest point in order to reach their highest point." Crucibles, the toughest moments of our professional and personal lives, have the potential to "contribute to us being part of something greater than ourselves," Dana says.

As she glances back to take in the whole of her leadership experiences, Dana acknowledges that life can be challenging, far more so than she ever thought growing up. But in the next breath, she says, "There's resolve in each of us." Although it was difficult to leave the Air Force and its mission, I wonder if Dana hasn't discovered her own, one where education and leadership, although admitted passions, are vehicles for putting trial to use. And I wonder if that inclination toward finding a larger context for life's challenges, for contribution, even in the midst of turmoil, isn't both her resolve and her mission.

Featured Narrative: Glen Tullman, CEO, Livongo Health, and Managing Partner, 7 Wire Ventures

I think we've got to understand we're creating a future every day.

Sometimes you have to bet the company. You're in a race against time, to get to market, to meet an anticipated shift, to stay ahead of technology. And those times, Glen Tullman tells me, are scary. When the former CEO of Allscripts left in 2012, he'd grown the company to more than 1.4 billion dollars in revenue from a starting line of less than 50 million. He'd bet wisely, having created substantial success from significant risk. When I interviewed him in his new seat as CEO of Livongo Health, he was starting over. That, he said, was a little scary, too.

There are two critical junctures in the life of a company, Glen tells me. One is at the beginning when you're in a fight for survival, the other comes later when you attempt to leverage for success. They are equally crucial, requiring an intense focus. But they are distinct. And Glen has seen his way through both. With a knowing laugh, he says, "Either one can kind of kill you." Survival requires money, sales, quality processes, and really good people. But that just means you're up and running, you've got your head above water. Success requires something altogether different because it asks different questions: How do we take this to the next level? How do we become the industry leader?

In an ideal world, you and your team grow as the company grows. There's time for iteration, for experimentation, for practicing. And in that context, leaders can foster a "very rapid kind of learning environment,"

Glen explains, one in which mistakes are made and shared. Google and Facebook, for example, are known for constantly learning from their users, for experimenting with what works and what doesn't, he says. But on occasion, there is a deficit of time. "In some cases, you no longer have the luxury of saying we're going to do these things small," Glen tells me. Looking back on his tenure as CEO of Allscripts, when they were trying to get electronic prescribing into the hands of doctors, he says, "We just believed that we had to take a substantial amount of risk because we thought the world was changing. We were very fortunate that we got those right. Most of the time."

But what's required for the survival of the CEO, for the person under whose guidance and leadership the future of the company resides, I wonder? What's needed to face the enormity of the responsibility and the risk? Without a moment's hesitation, Glen says, "You have to have a tremendous amount of perseverance and energy." He describes being CEO as an increasingly challenging role, if for no other reason than the world has become 24 × 7. There are so many audiences: employees, shareholders, the board. Self-confidence is a must. "You're making tough decisions, and the reality is you can't go to your board and say, 'I just don't know,'" he explains. And in the midst of the pressures and deadlines, incredibly important is also the ability to make the "right, values-based decisions," he shares.

"It can be a very lonely position," Glen says candidly. More than 12 of the people who worked for him at Allscripts went on to become CEOs, something he takes great pride in. And almost without exception, the most common thing he hears from those executives now is that they had no idea what he was dealing with, even when they thought they saw the whole picture, confirming that the responsibility of the role can be isolating. And in addition to the stewardship of the company is the leadership of its people. He says,

> You have to be able to digest every day and you have to be able to go home and sleep and come back the next day and deal with that again and inspire the people because a big part of leadership is also inspirational.

And that requires that CEOs recognize that they can't do it all, that in addition to inspiration, they must be strategic and set direction.

Delegation of what Glen describes as "real responsibilities" is essential, and for entrepreneurs, this can be particularly challenging. With a knowing chuckle, he tells me that "one of the blessings of growth is there is no other way to do that. No matter how many hours you have, you run out of hours when you get to a certain size."

What, then, takes a CEO to sustained performance? To the other side of survival and to success? As we talk about his experience as chief executive, about serving as Chancellor to the International Board of the Juvenile Diabetes Research Foundation, about investing significant amounts of his family foundation's money in the artificial pancreas project, it strikes me that these roles serve as opportunities for Glen, channels, for a much greater ambition. When he decided to choose Livongo as the place where he'd make that scary, new start, it was because the company was part of a larger picture, one in which, he says, "We're going to make a lot of different investments, but this one just felt like we could make a real difference in people's lives, and especially those who are underserved." The further we delve into his work and leadership, the more it becomes clear that Glen has deliberately applied his strengths and skills and talents, the whole of which would likely enable him to succeed anywhere as a CEO, to two gigantic social problems.

"Healthcare and education, these are the two fundamental problems of our country and our generation," Glen says emphatically. And he feels lucky to work in both, to attempt to make a real impact at scale. As we talk about his efforts, he can't contain his enthusiasm for some of the projects that he's attached to: cell towers that are reducing mortality rates among children, kids who had behavior problems in the classroom but are now engaged and learning through interactive sight, sound, and motion software, and Livongo's reason for being—to empower people living with chronic diseases to live better. Glen recognizes that other CEOs may not have the good fortune to work in these two important arenas and is quick to acknowledge that there are many important challenges that need attention. He points out that in addition to the fulfillment that he gains from working on these social challenges, the other area where he likes to see progress is the growth of people. And although it was deeply gratifying to see so many of his team go on to become CEOs, he's also invigorated by "seeing young people start to realize their dream," as they enter into his organization.

As he takes a wide-angle view of his work and leadership, of what he'd tell young people entering the workforce, Glen shares the importance of having diverse experiences, of volunteering, and of exploring some of the world. He talks about passion and doing what you love, that if you're really exceptional at something, it's amazing how you can be financially successful, and that true success is measured by one's happiness. He qualifies that as important as passion is, it requires effort, and that while there are stories of overnight success, those are unique and rare. He describes giving back as an essential quality and core value, one that he cultivates in himself and those who work for him, and emphasizes that, in addition to contribution, a connection to making a difference sustains everyone in an organization through the tough times. Citing Allscripts as an example, he recalls, "When we did electronic prescribing, we could calculate the number of peoples' lives that we saved from introducing our technology."

It's during the final moments of our conversation when I wonder if Glen doesn't capture, with simple precision, his sustained success as a CEO: "It's hard work, but it's worth it," he says.

Yes, running companies, leading people, taking risks, starting over, these are big things, often difficult things.

But the challenges of health care and education are, as well. And they ask that leaders be bigger.

CHAPTER 9

Creating Your Own Magnificent Leadership®: Practical Application

In this chapter, you'll find questions that correspond to each of the key factors for Magnificent Leadership®. They are organized by chapter and by leadership of self and leadership of others. You'll also find a worksheet on The Three Fuel Lines of Magnificent Leadership®.

Chapter 1: Passion Married to a High Tolerance for Uncertainty
Self-Leadership

1. What would you show up for at the kitchen table if no one were watching?
2. What makes you want to go "all in"?
3. What is the best expression of your talents, passions, and abilities, and how can you bring that to your work?
4. When there is a bruising disappointment, when the project flounders, the market shifts, or the client reconsiders, how would you fill in the sentence "Well, at least I still get to . . ."
5. When you've experienced significant uncertainty and limbo, what skills have you used to effectively navigate and tolerate that discomfort?

Leadership of Others

1. Is your team passionate about the work and mission of your organization? Are they "all in"?
2. Do you accept that for your organization to get substantially better, it must sometimes fail?
3. Have you assessed what you're willing to risk to move forward, and have you established measures, guardrails, and timelines?

4. When things don't go as planned, are you able to lead your team to bounce back with determination, fortitude, and passion?

5. Do you recognize the times when your business is most uncertain, and do you provide additional leadership during those periods so that your team can maintain its creativity and productivity?

Chapter 2: The Lens We Look Through: Framing and Reframing
Self-Leadership

1. Do you practice and cultivate the lens you look through and frame the challenges in your life in such a way that acknowledges the pain but also asks what you might do with that challenge, how you can use it?

2. Do you push yourself to try new experiences? Which experiences have given you more confidence or tapped skills that you didn't know you had, and how can you get more of those?

3. Do you have a "mantra" that is meaningful to you, one that gives comfort and orients you toward what is possible, even during very difficult times?

4. Are there talents that you have that were sparked by difficulty?

5. If you were to make a bet on yourself, what would it be?

Leadership of Others

1. Do you take it upon yourself as a leader to provide context for both challenge and success to your employees?

2. Do you find ways to convey to employees that their work matters and make that feedback as specific as possible?

3. Does your organization have a story of success that came from challenge and is it part of the culture?

4. Do you hire people who are interested in taking the journey with your organization? Who are able to ride the roller coaster of business with resilience?

5. Are performance reviews aspirational rather than punitive? Are they regarded as a way for already great team members to continue to grow? And do you set the tone by going first?

Chapter 3: Accepting What Is to Create What Can Be
Self-Leadership

1. What helps you to see opportunity and possibility when circumstances change?
2. Are you able to change with the times in ways that are important to your own vitality?
3. Do you consider habits or behaviors that may no longer serve you and do you have a way to change them if you so decide?
4. During tumult and upheaval, do you focus your energy and attention on what you can control, including your perspective? And do you simultaneously give yourself permission to feel the loss of the change?
5. Can you think of a time when you've successfully used and applied the formula "Acceptance + Focus on Possibility + Action = Living Courage" in your own life? What did you do, and what can you do to replicate your thinking and actions?

Leadership of Others

1. Do you prioritize weekly strategic thinking time of at least an hour to reflect on and observe change and to stay ahead of the curve in business?
2. Do you hire people who show an ability and comfort with adapting? Who demonstrate creativity, rather than resistance, in the face of change?
3. As a leader, do you encourage new ideas and projects for team members?
4. Are you building a flexible, adaptable organization capable of changing with the times in the key areas of client needs, markets, technology, brand, and competition?
5. Are your initiatives reactive or future focused and strategic?

Chapter 4: Magnificence Is Not a Solo Journey: Finding Someone to Hold the Vision
Self-Leadership

1. Do you have someone with whom you can talk about your hopes and dreams? Whom you trust to talk with about your fears and doubts?

2. If not, can you challenge yourself to approach people in your current circles, personal and professional, to have a mutually supportive relationship where each holds the vision for the other?

3. In the meantime, can you recall a special teacher, mentor, clergy member, family member, colleague, or friend who saw something in you that you did not see in yourself? Can you use that recollection to assist you in whatever your current pursuits are, to bolster your fortitude, perseverance, and belief in yourself?

4. Who do you most often surround yourself with? Do they believe in you and want the best for you? Do they celebrate your success? Are they able to provide comfort in defeat?

5. Did someone once see an opportunity for you that you did not see for yourself, or didn't feel ready for, that you would consider exploring now? Do you have a vision for your overall success that is bigger than your current accomplishments? Something that means a great deal to you?

Leadership of Others

1. Have you revisited the mission and vision of your organization to ensure that it's relevant and meaningful?

2. Is your mission and vision part of your daily work and are you and your team deeply connected to it?

3. Do you strive to see the potential of those who work for you? To nourish, encourage, and suggest stretch opportunities for your team members? Do you use specificity of praise when giving feedback to team members to encourage and reward excellence?

4. Do you use performance reviews as opportunities to discuss what employees are curious about or interested in taking on? Where they can grow and learn?

5. Do you have a culture of "finding the work around" when things get tough? One that encourages problem solving?

Chapter 5: Undaunted: Stretching Through Fear
Self-Leadership

1. What do you love so much, feel so committed to, that you're willing to be scared for it?

2. When circumstances have been daunting, what's worked to get you to stretch anyway?

3. What do you tell yourself when you're up against a big challenge? Is it a narrative that's helpful to accomplishing your goals?

4. What are the talents, skills, and gifts that you bring to any situation that, when applied, allow you to persevere? Are you able to draw on them during times of challenge?

5. Do you have the skills and tools necessary for gaining confidence and decisiveness in a new role and assuming the mantle of leadership? If you are aiming for a promotion, are you aware of what skills you'll need in the new role, and do you have a plan for either learning or bolstering them? Are you comfortable asking for help and guidance?

Leadership of Others

1. Do you create opportunities for communicating with your direct reports and all of the employees in your organization? Do you have vehicles for information to travel, from you to your team and from the front lines of the organization to you?

2. Is your team capable of meeting current and future needs in the organization? Or are there holes that need to be filled? Have you assessed your bench strength recently?

3. Are you able to inspire and lead your team and organization through trial? And do you have someone whom you trust that you can go to for guidance and perspective?

4. Do you support your team members in stretching their capabilities, and do you have a development program for up-and-coming leaders? Are you actively developing leaders at all levels in your organization? Is leadership development part of the culture? Aspirational?

5. Do you have core beliefs and values as a leader, team, and organization that are guiding principles and are relied upon when the waters get choppy to guide you in decision-making?

Chapter 6: Focusing On Success While Remaining Open to Iteration
Self-Leadership

1. Do you have meaningful goals that you want to achieve, or are you on autopilot?

2. Are you asking yourself and listening deeply about your aspirations and whether they're still right for you?

3. If they are, do you have a plan for going after them? If they're not, do you have someone with whom to talk about discovering and uncovering what you want?

4. On your path, are you open to what presents itself, to new information and insights? To altering the plan?

5. Do you create opportunities to experiment and explore, and dip your toe in the water?

Leadership of Others

1. Do you regularly discuss with your team members their individual goals, short and long term, and why they're important to them? Do you together review their action plans with measures and milestones?

2. Is your organization's strategy aspirational and in alignment with who you are as a leader and the mission of the organization?

3. Is your organization's strategy breathable? Is it built to be flexible if circumstances dictate?

4. Does your strategy have buy-in from key stakeholders, agreed-upon measures and check-ins, definitions of success, milestones, and a deep and thorough understanding about its importance and meaning to all involved?

5. Is your strategy designed to take into account the daily rigors and demands of all who are responsible for its execution? Has the strategy been made a priority?

Chapter 7: Questing for Self-Mastery
Self-Leadership

1. Do you know what it feels like to be centered and grounded in your own being and principles? Are you able to pause under stressful situations, even for a moment, to choose your response? Do you know how to find your way back when you've drifted from your center? Are you able to effectively prioritize under pressure?

2. Do you have thinking space and time away from the pressures and cacophony of the daily grind? Time to think strategically, to look at

the bigger picture? Do you have a trusted guide with whom you can talk about your aspirations, challenges, and successes? Someone who can help you magnify your strengths and value to your team and organization?

3. Are you cultivating a lifelong approach to learning? And are you pursuing relationships with peers and outside resources to broaden your perspective and thinking?

4. Do you use your success and achievement for ever-increasing learning and mastery? Do you continue to pursue challenges?

5. Do you extend your quest for mastery and learning to the work of leadership, itself, always striving to use your talents and abilities to their highest and best use in the context of leading?

Leadership of Others

1. Do you regard yourself as a learner as well as a leader, and does your team know that you don't have all of the answers all of the time? Do you own up to your mistakes and to being fallible?

2. Do you have a decision-making process that allows for gathering all of the information? Do you encourage, expect, and reward dissent? Do you have checks and balances for your decisions that include, whenever possible, time to take a step back?

3. Do you actively work to establish trust, creating open communication with your team, demonstrating transparency and empathy, being of support and having an open door, and being accessible for questions and ideas? Do you have your own version of "Listening Tours" so you can hear what's going on in your organization?

4. Do you encourage autonomy and responsibility in your team members, trusting them to do their jobs and being available for support and backup when needed? Do you provide a safety net if they should falter or have questions? Do you push them to excel but not to their detriment? Do you delegate important items and initiatives to your direct reports?

5. Do you believe that people who challenge your thinking make you more robust as a leader and more competitive on the whole as an organization? Do you value all opinion, even if it's new and not seasoned, thereby mitigating the possibility of a "halo bias"?

Chapter 8: A Connection to Contribution: Creating a Footprint
Self-Leadership

1. What do you want your footprint to say about you? About why you are here?

2. What do you feel most called or compelled to lend your time to?

3. Who are the people that matter most to you? The activities? Are you spending your time proportionate to their meaning?

4. Do you have a way to make meaning in times of challenge? To find a bigger context?

5. What is the work that sustains you the most, that gives you back more energy than it takes, even when you're working really hard? What fulfills you, helps to buoy you in times of pressure?

Leadership of Others

1. What do you find meaningful about leadership, and are you spending your time, effort, and energy connected to it? Are you merely surviving as a leader? Or have you achieved sustained performance and success?

2. If you were to lead others the way the best leader that you ever had led you, what would that look like? How would you behave?

3. Is a sense of meaning and contribution imbued throughout your organization, from the front lines to the top? Are regular updates communicated?

4. When your organization faces tough times, does everyone know what they're fighting for? Do you use a connection to contribution as a rallying cry? Are you regularly communicating why the work of the organization matters?

5. As a leader, what is the future that you want to create? For yourself, your team, your organization, and society?

The Three Fuel Lines of Magnificent Leadership®

There are three fuel lines that sustain us on the path of Magnificent Leadership®. While the questions in this worksheet are designed for those who are leading in organizations, the three fuel lines are equally important and applicable to self-leadership.

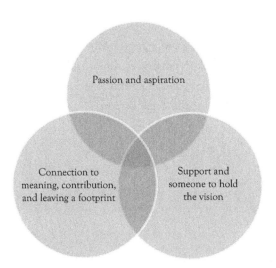

1. **Passion and Aspiration**
   - What excites and invigorates you about your work?
   - What do you so love doing that you would do it if no one were watching? When things are challenging, what do you still love returning to in your work?
   - Have you identified how to leverage that passion for yourself, your team, and your organization to drive business results?
2. **A Connection to Meaning, Contribution, and Leaving a Footprint**
   - What is the impact of what you do in your work? Consider all aspects of your leadership role and its ripple-out effect. Where

do you most derive satisfaction? Do you spend enough time there?

- Do you regularly connect your team members to the impact of their work and give context and meaning to their contributions, particularly when things are challenging?
- Is the mission and vision of your organization lived, breathed, and believed throughout your organization? Does the execution in your organization meet its guiding principles?

3. **Support and Someone to Hold the Vision**

- Do you have someone who holds the vision of your excellence and aspiration, who encourages you to be better and wants to see you fly?
- Do you have support for when things get challenging? Where you can let your guard down?
- How do you seek to preserve, sustain, and protect your own inspiration so that you can continue to inspire others on your team and in your organization?

About the Author

Sarah Levitt is the leading authority on Magnificent Leadership®, and is regularly invited to work with the world's most talented leaders, helping them to optimize their performance within chaotic, high-stakes environments. A trusted and strategic guide, Sarah brings penetrating insight, wit, and more than 20 years of practical business experience to her work with CEOs, corporate executives of Fortune 1000 companies, and senior leadership teams.

Sarah created The Making Magnificence Project®, an ongoing initiative, where she interviews successful leaders across different domains to capture their leadership journeys. Her book, *Magnificent Leadership*®, distills the essential elements of leadership success that she gleaned from these interviews.

Sarah is an international keynote speaker at conferences and leadership summits, including the American Bankers Association, Blue Cross Blue Shield, Ignite Leadership Summit, National Association of CEOs, and BASF. She has been a guest speaker at Harvard Kennedy School of Government's Center for Public Leadership.

Sarah is a columnist for *The Financial Manager* and was recruited to coach in the elite Executive MBA program at The University of North Carolina Kenan-Flagler business school.

She lives in Raleigh, North Carolina.

Index

OTHER TITLES IN THE HUMAN RESOURCE MANAGEMENT AND ORGANIZATIONAL BEHAVIOR COLLECTION

- *Slow Down to Speed Up: Lead, Succeed, and Thrive in a 24/7 World* by Liz Bywater
- *Agile Human Resources: Creating a Sustainable Future for the HR Profession* by Kelly Swingler
- *Infectious Innovation: Secrets of Transforming Employee Ideas Into Dramatic Revenue Growth* by James Allan
- *21st Century Skills for Non-Profit Managers: A Practical Guide on Leadership and Management* by Don Macdonald and Charles Oham
- *Conflict First Aid: How to Stop Personality Clashes and Disputes from Damaging You or Your Organization* by Nancy Radford
- *How to Manage Your Career: The Power of Mindset in Fostering Success* by Kelly Swingler
- *Deconstructing Management Maxims, Volume I: A Critical Examination of Conventional Business Wisdom* by Kevin Wayne
- *Deconstructing Management Maxims, Volume II: A Critical Examination of Conventional Business Wisdom* by Kevin Wayne
- *The Real Me: Find and Express Your Authentic Self* by Mark Eyre
- *Across the Spectrum: What Color Are You?* by Stephen Elkins-Jarrett
- *The Human Resource Professional's Guide to Change Management: Practical Tools and Techniques to Enact Meaningful and Lasting Organizational Change* by Melanie J. Peacock
- *Tough Calls: How to Move Beyond Indecision and Good Intentions* by Linda D. Henman

Announcing the Business Expert Press Digital Library

Concise e-books business students need for classroom and research

This book can also be purchased in an e-book collection by your library as

- a one-time purchase,
- that is owned forever,
- allows for simultaneous readers,
- has no restrictions on printing, and
- can be downloaded as PDFs from within the library community.

Our digital library collections are a great solution to beat the rising cost of textbooks. E-books can be loaded into their course management systems or onto students' e-book readers.
The **Business Expert Press** digital libraries are very affordable, with no obligation to buy in future years. For more information, please visit **www.businessexpertpress.com/librarians**. To set up a trial in the United States, please email **sales@businessexpertpress.com**.

CPSIA information can be obtained
at www.ICGtesting.com
Printed in the USA
LVOW13s1809220318
570811LV00014B/1148/P